Writing About Literature and Film

Writing About

LITERATURE

and FILM

Margaret B. Bryan

Boyd H. Davis

University of North Carolina, Charlotte

Harcourt Brace Jovanovich, Inc.

New York Chicago San Francisco Atlanta

WRITING ABOUT LITERATURE AND FILM

ISBN: 0-15-597854-3

Library of Congress Catalog Card Number: 75-3528

Printed in the United States of America

ACKNOWLEDGMENTS

*For permission to use the selections reprinted in this book, the authors are grateful to the
following publishers and copyright holders:*

ALISON M. K. BISHOP For Petrarch's "Sonnet" from *Love Rimes of Petrarch* by
Morris Bishop.

J. M. DENT & SONS LTD. For "The Hand That Signed the Paper" from *Collected
Poems* by Dylan Thomas. Reprinted by permission of J. M. Dent & Sons Ltd. and the
Trustees for the Copyrights of the late Dylan Thomas.

ROBERT WATERS GREY For "Search for Victims" by Robert Waters Grey. Copyright
1973 by Robert Waters Grey. Reprinted by permission.

HARCOURT BRACE JOVANOVICH, INC. For "Buffalo Bill's" by E. E. Cummings, copyright
1923, 1951, by E. E. Cummings, reprinted from his volume *Complete Poems 1913–1962;*
for "Women" from "In These Dissenting Times" by Alice Walker, © 1971 by Alice
Walker, reprinted from her volume *Revolutionary Petunias and Other Poems;* and for
"A Worn Path" by Eudora Welty, copyright 1941, 1969, by Eudora Welty, reprinted
from her volume *A Curtain of Green and Other Stories.* All reprinted by permission of
Harcourt Brace Jovanovich, Inc.

HARPER & ROW, PUBLISHERS, INC. For "We Real Cool" from *The World of Gwendolyn Brooks* (1971) by Gwendolyn Brooks. Copyright © 1959 by Gwendolyn Brooks
Blakely. By permission of Harper & Row, Publishers, Inc.

HARVARD UNIVERSITY PRESS For "I Like to See It Lap the Miles" by Emily Dickinson. Reprinted by permission of the publishers and the Trustees of Amherst College
from *The Poems of Emily Dickinson,* Thomas H. Johnson, Editor, Cambridge, Mass.:
The Belknap Press of Harvard University Press, copyright, 1951, 1955, by the President
and Fellows of Harvard College.

HOLT, RINEHART AND WINSTON, INC. For "Fire and Ice" and "Once by the Pacific"
from *The Poetry of Robert Frost,* edited by Edward Connery Lathem. Copyright 1923,
1928, © 1969 by Holt, Rinehart and Winston, Inc. Copyright 1951, © 1956 by Robert
Frost. Reprinted by permission of Holt, Rinehart and Winston, Publishers.

ALFRED A. KNOPF, INC. For "Domination of Black" by Wallace Stevens. Copyright
1923 and renewed 1951 by Wallace Stevens. Reprinted from *The Collected Poems of
Wallace Stevens,* by permission of Alfred A. Knopf, Inc.

MACMILLAN PUBLISHING COMPANY, INC. For "New England" from *Collected Poems* by
Edwin Arlington Robinson, copyright 1925 by Edwin Arlington Robinson, renewed 1953
by Ruth Nivison and Barbara R. Holt; and for "The Magi" from *Collected Poems* by
William Butler Yeats, copyright 1916 by Macmillan Publishing Co., Inc., renewed 1944
by Bertha Georgie Yeats. Both reprinted with permission of Macmillan Publishing
Co., Inc.

TO THE INSTRUCTOR

This book originated in the classroom. It began several years ago in the form of handouts for our students, whose questions and suggestions helped us to rework, refine, and eventually revise the handouts into the separate sections we present here. Friends and colleagues in high schools, community colleges, colleges, and universities provided more suggestions when they tested sections with their own classes.

Our book is an effort to help the student bridge the gap between the ability to read a work of literature or view a film, and the ability to write about the work with some confidence. The four genres we have chosen are poetry, short fiction, drama, and film. In each section, we have extracted elements basic to interpreting the genre and have presented them in a series of steps. Those steps are part of a process of analysis designed to stimulate another process: that of critical thought. The steps deal with those fundamental aspects of literary and cinematic genre which precede more sophisticated interpretation. Thus the literary and cinematic terminology used is not—indeed, cannot be—either definitive or comprehensive. Most of the examples we have selected—poems, stories, plays—are fairly short.

The last step in each section focuses specifically on types of writing that employ the analytic techniques discussed in the preceding steps. In our discussions of writing, we keep to six basic patterns or types: analysis of a single aspect of the work, analysis of multiple aspects, comparison and contrast, explication, exploration of a problem, and evaluation. Each type is illustrated by one or more undergraduate themes, two to a section.

Suggested topics for writing follow the student themes. These topics are arranged by type or pattern of writing, and each topic is keyed (where applicable) to the analytic step that the student must have mastered to write a paper on that topic. A brief checklist of documentation techniques follows the last section.

By this arrangement, we make possible at least three ways of using the book. It can be used as a self-contained introductory textbook, in which each step of each section can be the subject of a class session; nearly every step is accompanied, either within the section or in its list of writing topics, by at least one suggested writing assignment. The book can also be used to accompany literature anthologies, filmscripts, or series of films. Finally, the book can be used in an individualized, self-paced format, since each "step" involves comprehension of an analytic technique.

For their helpful comments on the manuscript, we would like to thank John R. Clark of the University of South Florida; Selwyn Kittredge of Fairleigh Dickinson University; and Susan Passler of Georgia State University. We would also like to thank these colleagues for their assistance: Jack Beasley, Ann Carver, Julian Mason, Catherine Nicholson, Byron Petrakis, Mary Stauffer, and John Wrigley of the University of North Carolina at Charlotte; Ruth Ann Fogartie of Central Piedmont Community College; and Charles Hadley of Queens College. Finally, we are grateful to the students who permitted us to reprint their papers in this book: Elizabeth Bryan, Eugenia Collins, Randall Crotts, Ren Decatur, Shannon Dudney, Gloria McGettigan, Bill Newman, and Sally Young.

Margaret B. Bryan
Boyd H. Davis

TO THE STUDENT

When you read a poem or short story, or see a film or play, you respond in some way to it. Frequently you will be asked—or will want—to discuss your response. Sometimes the discussion is oral; other times, you write about your responses in a journal, a letter, or an essay. But no matter what form the discussion takes, it isn't enough just to say you liked or disliked the work: you need to analyze the work and your response to it, first for yourself and then for others. The more precise and articulate you can make your analysis, the more effectively you can clarify and communicate your feelings, opinions, and judgments.

To analyze something means that you assume it to be a whole made up of parts and processes; this is true whether you are analyzing a lay-up shot in a basketball game, a mended wall, or a short story. Your analysis must be in terms of the work itself: a comment about carburetors makes very little sense if you are buying a tire. And your analysis is more explicit and effective if you know some of the names or terms appropriate either to a part of the creation you are examining or to the sort of analysis you are performing: a direction such as "Connect that squiggly thing sticking out to the bumpy blop there" is not as helpful as "Plug the speaker jack into its outlet."

Will a close analysis of all the parts ruin your appreciation of the play, the film, the story, the poem? No more than a careful study of Jack Nicklaus' drive or Chris Evert's backhand will prevent you from enjoying the U.S. Open or the Wimbledon Finals. We have all learned that "the whole is greater than the sum of its parts," and a part of the whole of any work is you and your response to it.

This book has been written to help you get past that numbing moment when you realize that while one may be perfectly able to read a literary work or view a film, and to appreciate, experience, and understand it on several levels, writing about that experience is a different matter.

We assume that you have available any one of a number of excellent glossaries, analytic studies, and anthologies, and that you have already begun your study of a particular genre or genres; so we have provided only brief definitions of a minimal number of terms.

We have broken up the process of writing about literature and film into a number of "steps." Your appreciation and understanding of an imaginative work can be developed by following these specific procedures for recording your impressions, feelings, opinions, and judgments. Of course, not every step will apply to the particular work—or even to a specific aspect of the work—that you have chosen to study and write about. Yet as you try to determine whether the step does apply, you may develop further insights of your own.

We are sure that you will soon be able to adapt this process to your own ends, and to progress beyond its modest scope.

Margaret B. Bryan
Boyd H. Davis

Contents

SECTION IV Analyzing and Writing About a Film 152

Writing About Literature and Film

Section I
Analyzing
and Writing
About a
POEM

Compared with other literary forms, poems are relatively brief. In a few lines a poet may distill the experiences of a decade, reveal the unsuspected depth in a familiar situation, or evoke a new dimension of an emotion such as love or grief. The careful analysis of a poem deepens and extends your understanding, which in turn helps to clarify your reaction to it. Each step that follows is designed to help you analyze a poem and your response to it, and to begin writing about it.

STEP 1

READ THE POEM CAREFULLY

To ensure that you read the poem carefully, write or type it out word for word; using double spacing, copy the space and line patterns of the original. This copy of the poem will be your worksheet. As ideas occur to you in your examination of the poem, jot them in the margins. Save the spaces between lines for other notes you will make later, in Steps 3 and 4. You may wish to copy the following poem and apply the various steps to your copy; you can then compare your worksheet with the illustrations from student worksheets reproduced in this discussion.

Search for Victims

Accustomed to violent storms, they found
no precedents dictating that the creak
of wind in the eaves and the pop of raindrops bound
for roots were more than that, until creeks
brawled from their gutters like drunks. Mountains lost
their faces. Boards, tin, bones, all dispossessed shreds
of human existence smashed across
to the gorged river, which rocked from its bed
through roads and bridges, wielding uprooted trees
like battering rams.
              There will be time to live
when scars heal, time for townsmen to increase
their knowledge, if their flesh is sensitive:
they search, below flood-exhumed tissues tossed
to trees, from which they droop like Spanish moss.

        Robert Waters Grey (1943-   )

STEP 2

DECIDE WHAT THE POEM IS ABOUT

Jot down very briefly what you think the poem is about—death, love, flowers, a woman's smile. Think of this idea as a sort of title, or headline, for your next task: a prose paraphrase of the poem. Write in prose a restatement of the poem, section by section or line by line. Try to make your sentence structure parallel that of the original. A headline and a paraphrase for "Search for Victims" might be something like this:

STORM, FLOOD, AND DEATH

Since they were used to terrible storms, nothing in their experience warned them that the wind that made the eaves creak and the sound of raindrops on the roof (roof tin?), welcome in their promise of green grass and trees, might be anything unusual, until the creeks overflowed. There were landslides in the mountains. Wreckage of houses and cars perhaps and bones of animals—or even people—were hurled down the swollen river, which flooded roads and wiped out bridges as though it were using the trees floating in it as battering rams.

There will be time to live again later when all the damage is repaired, time for people who live in towns to learn something you don't usually learn in the city, if they manage to maintain some sort of receptivity to the lesson the flood is giving them: right now they're searching for its victims underneath the trees, which are draped with dead bodies hanging from them like Spanish moss.

The poem you choose to analyze may use a fairly obvious method of organization, such as the "When I . . . When I . . . when I . . . then . . ." clauses in John Keats' "When I Have Fears." Your prose paraphrase should reflect or include that pattern:

When I Have Fears

When I have fears that I may cease to be
  Before my pen has gleaned my teeming brain,
Before high-piled books, in charact'ry,
  Hold like rich garners the full-ripened grain;
When I behold, upon the night's starred face,
  Huge cloudy symbols of a high romance,
And think that I may never live to trace
  Their shadows, with the magic hand of chance;

And *when I* feel, fair creature of an hour,
   That I shall never look upon thee more,
Never have relish in the faery power
   Of unreflecting love!—*then* on the shore
Of the wide world I stand alone, and think
Till Love and Fame to nothingness do sink.

      John Keats (1795–1821)

Sample Prose Paraphrase

When I am afraid that I might die before I have written down all my ideas or before my books hold the plentiful golden ideas I have; *when I* see in the starry night sky the huge clouds that symbolize romantic adventure and think I might not live long enough to follow out the magical adventures they promise; and *when I* feel, my mortal love, that I will never see you again or enjoy love for its own sake—*then* I stand on the edge of the world and think and think until the ideas of love and fame dissolve to nothingness.

Look now at the *way* the poem tells you something—that is, its *mode*. A poem that tells a story is in the *narrative mode*. A poem about somebody's feelings—about love or death or a spring day— uses the *lyric mode*. If the poem merely describes something, the mode is *descriptive*. If the poet has invented a character or *persona* who speaks the poem, the mode is *dramatic*. Obviously, a poem may be delivered in more than one mode; generally, however, one mode is dominant. Add a note about the mode of the poem to your paraphrase. For example, would "Search for Victims" be descriptive and narrative, with the descriptive mode predominating?

STEP 3

EXTEND YOUR UNDERSTANDING
OF THE POEM

Look carefully at your paraphrase: if you are still baffled by the poem, perhaps you are having trouble with unfamiliar words, unusual sentence structure, ambiguous or absent punctuation, or unfamiliar allusions.

If your problem is with unfamiliar words, use an unabridged dictionary to check all the possible meanings of these words. If a word with multiple meanings is used, decide whether the poet intends a deliberate *ambiguity*. In that case, more than one definition of the word is important to the poem. Does the deliberate ambiguity involve *irony,* which has been defined as "the simultaneous recognition of differing points of view"? * In the following poem, look at the multiple meanings of "sovereign" (a ruler, predominant, supreme, absolute) in connection with the "five kings," or fingers.

The Hand That Signed the Paper
Felled a City

The hand that signed the paper felled a city;
Five sovereign fingers taxed the breath,
Doubled the globe of dead and halved a country;
These five kings did a king to death.

The mighty hand leads to a sloping shoulder,
The finger joints are cramped with chalk;
A goose's quill has put an end to murder
That put an end to talk.

* Robert M. Wallace, Professor Emeritus, University of North Carolina at Charlotte.

The hand that signed the treaty bred a fever,
And famine grew, and locusts came;
Great is the hand that holds dominion over
Man by a scribbled name.

The five kings count the dead but do not soften
The crusted wound nor pat the brow;
A hand rules pity as a hand rules heaven;
Hands have no tears to flow.

Dylan Thomas (1914–1953)

If your problem with the poem is its unusual sentence structure, reshape the sentences into ordinary English. Then try to decide why the poet used the unusual word order—perhaps, for example, to emphasize certain words or phrases. In the following poem, look at the way "We" is emphasized at the ends of the lines until it disappears. Why do you think the "We" is missing from the last line?

We Real Cool

The Pool Players.
Seven at the Golden Shovel.

We real cool. We
Left school. We

Lurk late. We
Strike straight. We

Sing sin. We
Thin gin. We

Jazz June. We
Die soon.

Gwendolyn Brooks (1915–   )

The opening lines of John Milton's *Paradise Lost* can be reshaped into a sentence using normal word order:

From *Paradise Lost*

Of Man's First Disobedience, and the Fruit
Of that Forbidden Tree, whose mortal taste
Brought Death into the World, and all our woe,
With loss of *Eden,* till one greater Man
Restore us, and regain the blissful Seat,
Sing Heav'nly Muse, that on the secret top
Of *Oreb,* or of *Sinai,* didst inspire
That Shepherd, who first taught the chosen Seed,
In the Beginning how the Heav'ns and Earth
Rose out of *Chaos:* Or if *Sion* Hill
Delight thee more, and *Siloa's* Brook that flow'd
Fast by the Oracle of God; I thence
Invoke thy aid to my advent'rous Song,
That with no middle flight intends to soar
Above the *Aonian* Mount, while it pursues
Things unattempted yet in Prose or Rhyme.

John Milton (1608–1674)

Sing, Heavenly Muse, that on the secret top of Oreb or of Sinai didst inspire that Shepherd who first taught the chosen Seed in the beginning how the Heavens and Earth rose out of Chaos, of man's first disobedience and the Fruit of that Forbidden Tree whose mortal taste brought Death into the World and all our woe with loss of Eden till one greater Man restore us and regain the blissful Seat; or if Sion Hill and Siloa's Brook that flowed fast by the Oracle of God delight thee more, I thence invoke thy aid to my adventurous Song that with no middle flight intends to soar above the Aonian Mount while it pursues things unattempted yet in Prose or Rhyme.

If your problem is with ambiguous punctuation, or lack of punctuation, look to see whether the poem uses or omits punctuation in order to say more than one thing at a time. If you see that a phrase or clause can modify more than one part of its context, evaluate the resulting different meanings carefully. Perhaps the absence of punctuation throughout the following poem about Buffalo Bill underscores the continual presence of death; without punctuation, the final question could be, instead, ironic commentary.

Buffalo Bill's
defunct
     who used to
     ride a watersmooth-silver
              stallion
and break onetwothreefourfive pigeonsjustlikethat
                       Jesus

he was a handsome man
                and what i want to know is
how do you like your blueeyed boy
Mister Death

   e. e. cummings (1894–1962)

The poem may use *allusions* that you need to look up. Do all the allusions pertain to one area of reference, such as Greek mythology, the Roaring Twenties, the Wild West? The allusion to Helen of Troy is central to the meaning of Hilda Doolittle's "Helen"; you might write a paper explaining this.

Helen

All Greece hates
the still eyes in the white face,
the luster as of olives
where she stands,
and the white hands.

All Greece reviles
the wan face when she smiles,
hating it deeper still
when it grows wan and white,
remembering past enchantments
and past ills.

Greece sees unmoved,
God's daughter, born of love,
the beauty of cool feet
and slenderest knees,
could love indeed the maid,
only if she were laid,
white ash amid funereal cypresses.

H. D. (Hilda Doolittle, 1886–1961)

STEP 4

ANALYZE THE RHYME

Read the poem aloud and listen to the sounds. If you can clearly hear *end rhyme,* similar sounds at the ends of the lines, you can jot down a *rhyme scheme* beside your copy of the poem, using letters to indicate the different rhymes, as illustrated in the following poem:

Fire and Ice

Some say the world will end in fire,	*a*
Some say in ice.	*b*
From what I've tasted of desire	*a*
I hold with those who favor fire.	*a*
But if it had to perish twice,	*b*
I think I know enough of hate	*c*

To say that for destruction ice   *b*
Is also great   *c*
And would suffice.   *b*

Robert Frost (1874–1963)

What patterns of rhyme do you hear or see in your poem? For instance, a *couplet* is a two-line *stanza*, or section of verse, with the rhyme scheme *aa*. A *quatrain* is a four-line stanza; some of the most frequently used quatrains are the *heroic (abab)*, the *couplet (aabb)*, the *enclosing (abba)*, and the *ballad (abcb)*. A *sonnet* has fourteen lines: the *English*, or *Shakespearean, sonnet* consists of three quatrains and a couplet (usually *abab cdcd efef gg*); the *Italian*, or *Petrarchan, sonnet* consists of an *octave* (eight lines that are really two enclosing quatrains—*abba abbà*) and a *sestet* (six lines, often *cde cde, cd cd cd,* or a similar arrangement). Can you classify the following poem according to its rhyme scheme?

From *Astrophel and Stella: 31*

With how sad steps, Oh Moon, thou climb'st the skies,
How silently, and with how wan a face!
What, may it be that even in heav'nly place
That busy archer his sharp arrows tries?
Sure, if that long-with-love-acquainted eyes
Can judge of love, thou feel'st a lover's case;
I read it in thy looks: thy languished grace,
To me that feel the like, thy state descries.
Then even of fellowship, Oh Moon, tell me,
Is constant love deemed there but want of wit?
Are beauties there as proud as here they be?
Do they above love to be loved, and yet
Those lovers scorn whom that love doth possess?
Do they call virtue there ungratefulness?

Sir Philip Sidney (1554–1586)

True rhyme (rhyme that matches, like "moon" and "spoon") is not the only form of rhyming device that your poem may use.

Perhaps the words at the ends of the lines are similar in other ways. The poet may have used several devices to create a pattern, including *slant rhyme*—either *consonance,* in which the consonants in final words of two lines match but the preceding vowels are different, as in "prep*are*" and "l*ure*"; or *assonance,* in which the vowels match but the consonants differ, as in "c*oast*" and "t*orn*." Mark the lines in which these devices occur, and add notes on your worksheet where appropriate, as illustrated below:

Search for Victims

Section 1

Accustomed to violent storms, they found *a*

no precedents dictating that the [creak] *b*　*b - b not true: creak- creeks*

of wind in the eaves and the pop of raindrops *creeks*

bound　　　　　　　　　　　　　　*a*

for roots were more than that, until [creeks] *b*

brawled from their gutters like drunks.

Section 2

Mountains [lost]　　　　　　　*c*　*c-c not true: lost- across*

their faces. Boards, tin, bones, all dispossessed *across*

[shreds]　　　　　　　　　　*d*　*d-d not true: shreds- bed (s-sounds?)*

of human existence smashed [across] *c*

to the gorged river, which rocked from its [bed] *d*

through roads and bridges, wielding uprooted

[trees] *e*　　　　　　　*e-e not true: trees (-z)- increase (-s)*

like battering rams.

> There will be time to live **f**
>
> when scars heal, time for townsmen to [increase] **e**
>
> their knowledge, if their flesh is sensitive: **f**
>
> **Section 3** they search, below flood-exhumed tissues [tossed] g(c)
>
> to trees, from which they droop like Spanish
>
> [moss].
>
> *Robert Waters Grey*

g (c)
g-g (same as c)
not true
tossed - moss

Assonance, consonance, and other metrical devices such as *alliteration* (repeating the same sound at the start of several words) may be used in places other than the ends of lines; indicate such devices on your worksheet wherever they occur. The poet may have used *internal rhyme;* mark this with *I.R.* Make comments in the margins wherever appropriate. Here is a sample worksheet for "Search for Victims":

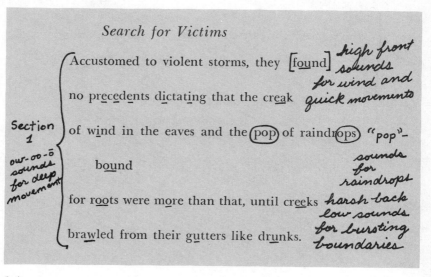

> *Search for Victims*
>
> Accustomed to violent storms, they [found] *high front sounds*
> *for wind and*
> no precedents dictating that the creak *quick movements*
>
> **Section 1** of wind in the eaves and the (pop) of raindrops) *"pop"—*
> *sounds for raindrops*
> *our-oo-ō sounds for deep movement* bound
>
> for roots were more than that, until creeks *harsh back low sounds*
>
> brawled from their gutters like drunks. *for bursting boundaries*

Mountains lost

their faces. [Boards], tin, [bones], all dispossessed

    shreds

hard s-sounds (next to hard consonants): cons. - for tearing

of human existence smashed across

to the [gorged] [river], which [rocked] from its [bed]

through [roads] and [bridges], wielding [uprooted]

    [trees]

like [battering] [rams].

r-cons. & r-allit. rock back and forth to each other - continual force

Section 2

b-allit.: boards bones bed bridges battering - all hard; they batter

There will be [time] to

    live

when scars heal, [time] for [townsmen] to

t-allit. with soft vowel

slows down movement - as does th-allit.

    increase

[their] knowledge, if [their] flesh is sensitive:

s-allit & s-cons. here is soft: next to vowels or soft consonants (except harsh "scars":

they search, below flood-exhumed [tissues] [tossed]

[to] [trees], from which [they] droop like Spanish

sk-sound.

    moss.

Scars are harsh, will heal.)

Section 3

Robert Waters Grey

Note contrasts of sight and sound imagery and of activity in three sections, to give before-and-after view.

Here is a poem by Gerard Manley Hopkins. A sample worksheet has been done for the first half of the poem; try your hand at analyzing the second half:

As Kingfishers Catch Fire, Dragonflies Draw Flame

Note interplay
line 1:
k-k-f rallit.
d-d-f
Closer illus-
tration of
parallel:
supported by
metrical
devices

I. R.
serves
similar
purpose
in connection
with
external
rhyme?

-ing
-ung } *sounds:*
I. R. only

As [kingfishers] [catch] [fire], [dragonflies] [dráw]

[fláme];

As tumbled over [rim] in [roundy] wells

I.R. ← → I.R.
Stones [ring]; like each tucked [string]

IR.
[tells], each hung [bell's]

I.R. ← → I.R.   I.R.
Bow [swung] finds [tongue] to [fling] out broad

   its name;

I.R. ← → I.R.
Each mortal [thing] does one [thing] and the

   same: ?   ?

Deals out that [being] indoors each one

   [dwells];

[Selves]—goes [itself]; [myself] it [speaks]
   s-allit.
and [spells],

Crying *Whát I dó is me: for that I came.*

Í say móre: the just man justices;

Kéeps gráce: thát keeps all his goings graces;

lines 6-7: ell-sounds internal
and external, compare -elf/-elves
assonance!

Acts in God's eye what in God's eye he is—

Christ—for Christ plays in ten thousand places,

Lovely in limbs, and lovely in eyes not his

To the Father through the features of men's

faces.

Gerard Manley Hopkins (1844–1889)

STEP 5

ANALYZE THE METER

The *meter* of a poem refers to its patterns of *stresses,* which are often connected with other aspects of the poem in ways that will be discussed later on. To analyze a poem's meter, first divide the words of the poem into syllables, checking the dictionary if you are unsure of your division; then read the poem aloud—several times, if necessary—in a normal conversational manner, listening for heavy and weak stresses. In English words with more than one syllable, the stresses on those syllables vary; for example, the word "paper" has a heavier stress on "pa" than on "per." Words of one syllable have a heavy or a light stress according to their context: in the phrase "a man of means," "a" and "of" have a lighter stress than "man" and "means."

In the spaces between the lines on your worksheet, mark each *heavy stress* with a "slash" /; mark each *weak stress* with a "sloop" ∪ . Do you see any recurrent patterns? Here is a marked worksheet of "Search for Victims"; look for stress patterns within the various sections of the poem:

Search for Victims

Accustomed to violent storms, they found

no precedents dictating that the creak

of wind in the eaves and the pop of raindrops bound

for roots were more than that, until creeks

brawled from their gutters like drunks. Mountains lost

their faces. Boards, tin, bones, all dispossessed shreds

of human existence smashed across

→ Six heavy stresses-like battering rams

to the gorged river, which rocked from its bed

through roads and bridges, wielding uprooted trees

like battering rams.

Note break-and emphasis on word "live"

          There will be time to live

When scars heal, time for townsmen to increase

their knowledge, if their flesh is sensitive:

they search, below flood-exhumed tissues tossed

to trees, from which they droop like Spanish moss.

Perfect iambic pentameter- calm after storm

Robert Waters Grey

Meter irregular — so is storm!
/ ∪ ∪ / ∪ ∪ for drunken creeks,
rocking rivers, battering
series of heavy stresses: line 6
last line regular: ∪ / ∪ / ∪ / ∪ / ∪ /

Patterns of stresses are called *feet*. The four most commonly used feet in English poetry are: the *iamb*, or *iambic foot* (‿ /); the *trochee*, or *trochaic foot* (/ ‿); the *anapest*, or *anapestic foot* (‿ ‿ /); and the *dactyl*, or *dactylic foot* (/ ‿ ‿). Does your poem tend to use one foot more than another? Is this true only of certain lines or of the whole poem? Mark what you discover on your worksheet.

Count the number of feet in each line to determine its meter. (There can be more than one type of foot in a line.) Most poems in English have lines of *pentameter* (five feet—that is, five heavy stresses—per line), *tetrameter* (four feet), or *trimeter* (three feet). Look closely at your poem, which you have *scanned*, or marked for feet. Does your poem have a general metrical pattern of any specific meter? Perhaps your poem's patterns are alternated: in many ballads, the lines of a stanza are alternated between tetrameter and trimeter. If you think that the rhyme, foot, or meter of a line contributes to the meaning of the poem in any way, note it on your worksheet.

If your poem has, in general, one predominant metrical pattern, see whether there are any sharp changes from it. You might use an asterisk (*) to mark such places. Think about the changes: does the poet want to emphasize certain words by changing word order or shifting meter? In the following poem, the meter shifts from tetrameter in the quatrain to heptameter and hexameter when the bugle blows and echoes answer:

The Splendor Falls on Castle Walls

The splendor falls on castle walls
    And snowy summits old in story;
The long light shakes across the lakes
    And the wild cataract leaps in glory.
Blow, bugle, blow, set the wild echoes flying,
Blow, bugle; answer, echoes, dying, dying, dying.

O hark, O hear! How thin and clear,
  And thinner, clearer, farther going!
O sweet and far from cliff and scar
  The horns of Elfland faintly blowing!
Blow, let us hear the purple glens replying,
Blow, bugle; answer, echoes, dying, dying, dying.

O love, they die in yon rich sky,
  They faint on hill or field or river;
Our echoes roll from soul to soul,
  And grow forever and forever.
Blow, bugle, blow, set the wild echoes flying,
And answer, echoes, answer, dying, dying, dying.

Alfred, Lord Tennyson (1809–1892)

Few poems are completely regular. Even within a poem that looks regular at first, you may find unexpected changes in foot or meter. Look at the heavy emphasis on the verbs in the second and fourth lines of the following sonnet. The first four lines have been scanned; mark the stresses in the rest of the poem.

Holy Sonnet: 14

Batter my heart, three-personed God; for You

As yet but knock, breathe, shine, and seek to mend;

That I may rise and stand, o'erthrow me, and bend

Your force to break, blow, burn, and make me new.

I, like an usurped town, to another due,

Labor to admit You, but O, to no end;

Reason, Your viceroy in me, me should defend,

But is captived, and proves weak or untrue.

Yet dearly I love You, and would be loved fain,

But am betrothed unto Your enemy.

Divorce me, untie or break that knot again;

Take me to You, imprison me, for I,

Except You enthrall me, never shall be free,

Nor ever chaste, except You ravish me.

John Donne (1572–1631)

The title of the following poem, "Stanzas for Music," helps to explain why a poem uses iambs, anapests, trochees: lyrics for songs are often poems. You might wish to analyze the meter of some modern lyrics.

Stanzas for Music (*There Be None of Beauty's Daughters*)

1

There be none of Beauty's daughters
  With a magic like thee;
And like music on the waters
  Is thy sweet voice to me:
When, as if its sound were causing
The charmed ocean's pausing,
The waves lie still and gleaming,
And the lulled winds seem dreaming;

And the midnight moon is weaving
  Her bright chain o'er the deep;
Whose breast is gently heaving,
  As an infant's asleep:
So the spirit bows before thee,
To listen and adore thee;
With a full but soft emotion,
Like the swell of summer's ocean.

George Gordon, Lord Byron (1788–1824)

STEP 6

ANALYZE THE LARGER PATTERNS

Foot, meter, and rhyme often combine into patterns, and some of them have been given names, such as *couplet, ballad,* and *sonnet.* We discussed their rhyme schemes in Step 4, and saw that some *stanza patterns* also require a certain number of lines. While a *couplet* consists of two lines—

Engraved on the Collar of a Dog, Which I Gave to His Royal Highness

I am his Highness' dog at Kew;
Pray tell me, sir, whose dog are you?

Alexander Pope (1688–1744)

—a poem may be one hundred lines long and made up of fifty couplets, or it may be of some other form combined with one couplet. A *tercet* is a three-line stanza. Note the silklike slithering of the *s*'s in the first tercet of the following poem:

Upon Julia's Clothes

Whenas in silks my Julia goes,
Then, then, methinks, how sweetly flows
That liquefaction of her clothes.

Next, when I cast mine eyes and see
That brave vibration, each way free,
O, how that glittering taketh me!

Robert Herrick (1591–1674)

Count the number of lines in the poem you are studying or the number of lines in its stanzas, if it has more than one. Count the stanzas, too: they frequently serve as *verse paragraphs*. Look at the number of lines in relation to your poem's rhyme scheme and metrical pattern. Some stanza patterns are linked to specific rhyme schemes or metrical patterns. A *ballad,* for example, is traditionally composed of *quatrains* rhyming *abcb,* in which the *a* and *c* lines are usually in tetrameter (four feet) and the *b* lines are in trimeter (three feet). Ballads often celebrate a particular cultural heritage while dealing with universal situations or emotions. When they tell a tale, the action may be only suggested, not described. The ballad that follows is an old one, but folk and country musicians still compose ballads in—and for—modern times.

Get Up and Bar the Door

1

It fell about the Martinmas * time,
   And a gay time it was then,
When our goodwife got puddings to make,
   And she's boiled them in the pan.

* *Martinmas:* the feast of St. Martin, November 11.

2

The wind sae cauld blew south and north,
    And blew into the floor;
Quoth our goodman to our goodwife,
    "Gae out and bar the door."

3

"My hand is in my hussyfskap,*
    Goodman, as ye may see;
An * it should nae be barred this hundred year,
    It s' * no be barred for me."

4

They made a paction 'tween them twa,
    They made it firm and sure,
That the first word whae'er should speak,
    Should rise and bar the door.

5

Then by there came two gentlemen,
    At twelve o'clock at night,
And they could neither see house nor hall,
    Nor coal nor candle-light.

6

"Now whether is this a rich man's house,
    Or whether is it a poor?"
But ne'er a word wad ane o' them speak,
    For barring of the door.

7

And first they ate the white puddings,
    And then they ate the black;
Though muckle * thought the goodwife to hersel,
    Yet ne'er a word she spak.

* *Hussyfskap:* housewifery; *An:* if; *s':* shall; *muckle:* much.

8

Then said the one unto the other,
  "Here, man, tak ye my knife;
Do ye tak aff the auld man's beard,
  And I'll kiss the goodwife."

9

"But there's nae water in the house,
  And what shall we do then?"
"What ails ye at * the pudding-broo,*
  That boils into the pan?"

10

O up then started our goodman,
  An angry man was he:
"Will ye kiss my wife before my een,*
  And scad * me wi' pudding-bree?" *

11

Then up and started our goodwife,
  Gied * three skips on the floor:
"Goodman, you've spoken the foremost word,
  Get up and bar the door."

Once we know that a poem is written in one of the standard
poetic forms, then we may be able to discover further clues about
the poem's overall structure. As we have seen, *sonnets* are traditionally fourteen lines of iambic pentameter. However, within
this form, a sonnet may be made up of three quatrains, each a
"paragraph" that concerns a different aspect of the subject (love,
for example), and a couplet that states a conclusion of some sort:

* *What ails ye at:* what's wrong with; *broo:* broth; *een:* eyes; *scad:* scald; *bree:* broth;
  Gied: gave.

Sonnet 116

Let me not to the marriage of true minds
Admit impediments. Love is not love
Which alters when it alteration finds,
Or bends with the remover to remove:

Love (neg. def.) doesn't change

O, no! it is an ever-fixèd mark
That looks on tempests and is never shaken;
It is the star to every wand'ring bark,
Whose worth's unknown, although his height be
    taken.

Love (pos.) remains constant

Love's not Time's fool, though rosy lips and cheeks
Within his bending sickle's compass come;
Love alters not with his brief hours and weeks,
But bears it out even to the edge of doom.

Love: unchanged by Time (3 diff. ways of saying something about Love's permanence)

  If this be error and upon me proved,
  I never writ, nor no man ever loved.

ironic: if I'm wrong, nobody ever loved

William Shakespeare (1564–1616)

Another sonnet's (eight-line) *octave* may be used to present an argument and its (six-line) *sestet* to present a refutation:

Sonnet CCXVII

Once I besought her mercy with my sighs,
Striving in love-rime to communicate
My pain, to see in that immaculate
Unmelting heart the fires of pity rise.
I longed, the freezing cloud that round her lies
In the eloquent winds of love to dissipate—
Or else I'd rouse against her all men's hate
Because she hid from me her lovely eyes.

Argument (Once I wanted all to hate her if she would not relent and love me)

But now I wish no longer hate for her,
Nor for me, pity; for I know at last
In vain against my fate I spend my breath.
Only I'll sing how she is lovelier
Than the divine, that, when my flesh is cast,
The world may know how happy was my death.

Petrarch (1304–1374)

Refutation (Now I don't want hatred and will be happy writing about her)

Like other patterns of organization, argument and refutation can be found in many types of poetry. A recurrent pattern of iambic pentameter lines without rhyme is called *blank verse*. The absence of any standard pattern indicates that the poet has used *free verse*. In the poems that follow, look for argument and refutation of a sort in "Memories of an Early Marriage"; follow the cat's movements in "The Pennycandystore Beyond the El."

Memories of an Early Marriage

I

Your body brown from the sun
is open to the sunlight as a peach
filled with the light and glowing its own color.
Your hair spreads softly on the pillow,
where you drowsily lie talking, wondering
a little on some question I can answer
only when I hold the sunlight warm
and clear as you are in my eyes.
I would like to be rewarded like the sun's light
that finds rebirth in you—itself again—
turned to flesh that glows like wisdom
in a face turned warm and smiling toward it.
Into your body goes the light, awakening
the life that lies there, hoping to be given birth.
Give forth light, then, and let the giving be
return for what it gave you, sun and life.

II

My dear, there is this lovely openness
in your outraged and silent hurt, that says
you do not need to blind me with your courage,
always reticent and warm, like sun
behind palms placed firmly on my eyes and held
until I speak those words that show I know you
more than all others who have so invoked
the silent struggle that brings recognition.

Paul B. Newman (1919–   )

The Pennycandystore Beyond the El

The pennycandystore beyond the El
is where I first
                fell in love
                        with unreality
Jellybeans glowed in the semi-gloom
of that september afternoon
A cat upon the counter moved among
                        the licorice sticks
                and tootsie rolls
        and Oh Boy Gum
Outside the leaves were falling as they died

A wind had blown away the sun

A girl ran in
Her hair was rainy
Her breasts were breathless in the little room

Outside the leaves were falling
                and they cried
                        Too soon! too soon!

Lawrence Ferlinghetti (1919–   )

STEP *7*

ANALYZE THE IMAGERY

Since poets must be concise—saying in a few words what would require many more words of prose—they use *images,* words or phrases that appeal to the senses. On your worksheet for your poem, underline any images you find, noting the sense or senses they appeal to. Then decide whether there is any pattern to the imagery. Perhaps the images come from a single area of reference (water, sounds, weather). If there is a shift from one area of reference to another, or a logical or chronological progression, look for possible reasons for the change. In Alice Walker's poem, note how the women's hands begin as fists, then open to lead and to nurture. In the poem by Frost, note how the imagery progresses from water to land, from anger to rage and the suggestion of doom.

Women

They were women then
My mama's generation
Husky of voice—Stout of
Step
With fists as well as
Hands
How they battered down
Doors
And ironed
Starched white
Shirts
How they led
Armies
Headragged Generals
Across mined
Fields

Booby-trapped
Ditches
To discover books
Desks
A place for us
How they knew what we
Must know
Without knowing a page
Of it
Themselves.

Alice Walker (1944-   )

Once by the Pacific

The shattered water made a misty din.
Great waves looked over others coming in,
And thought of doing something to the shore
That water never did to land before.
The clouds were low and hairy in the skies,
Like locks blown forward in the gleam of eyes.
You could not tell, and yet it looked as if
The shore was lucky in being backed by cliff,
The cliff in being backed by continent;
It looked as if a night of dark intent
Was coming, and not only a night, an age.
Someone had better be prepared for rage.
There would be more than ocean-water broken
Before God's last *Put out the Light* was spoken.

Robert Frost (1874-1963)

STEP 8

LOOK FOR RHETORICAL DEVICES

On your worksheet, note in the margins any rhetorical devices that are employed. With *apostrophe,* an absent person or an abstraction is addressed directly, as in

O Western Wind

O western wind, when wilt thou blow
    That the small rain down can rain?

Christ, that my love were in my arms,
    And I in my bed again.

    Anonymous

Simile and *metaphor* are both forms of comparison. With simile, "like" or "as" is used in comparing two objects, ideas, or persons, as in the Robert Burns poem below. With *metaphor,* a comparison is also made, but "like" or "as" is not used. Sometimes a metaphor is extended throughout the poem; in the poem by Emily Dickinson below, the train is pictured as an animal, which in the last stanza is seen to be a horse.

A Red, Red Rose

O, my luve is like a red, red rose,
    That's newly sprung in June.
O, my luve is like the melodie
    That's sweetly played in tune.

As fair art thou, my bonnie lass,
    So deep in luve am I,
And I will luve thee still, my dear,
    Till a' the seas gang dry.

Till a' the seas gang dry, my dear,
   And the rocks melt wi' the sun!
And I will luve thee still, my dear,
   While the sands o' life shall run.

And fare thee wel, my only luve,
   And fare thee wel awhile!
And I will come again, my luve,
   Though it were ten thousand mile!

     Robert Burns (1759–1796)

I Like to See It Lap the Miles

I like to see it lap the miles,
And lick the valleys up,
And stop to feed itself at tanks;
And then, prodigious, step

Around a pile of mountains,
And, supercilious, peer
In shanties by the sides of roads;
And then a quarry pare

To fit its ribs,
And crawl between,
Complaining all the while
In horrid, hooting stanza;
Then chase itself down hill

And neigh like Boanerges;
Then, punctual as a star,
Stop—docile and omnipotent—
At its own stable door.

     Emily Dickinson (1830–1886)

In *personification,* nonhuman forms, ideas, or objects are given human qualities. The old proverb "Curiosity killed the cat" is given new meaning in the following poem:

New England

Here where the wind is always north-north-east
And children learn to walk on frozen toes,
Wonder begets an envy of all those
Who boil elsewhere with such a lyric yeast
Of love that you will hear them at a feast
Where demons would appeal for some repose,
Still clamoring where the chalice overflows
And crying wildest who have drunk the least.

Passion is here a soilure of the wits,
We're told, and Love a cross for them to bear;
Joy shivers in the corner where she knits
And Conscience always has the rocking-chair,
Cheerful as when she tortured into fits
The first cat that was ever killed by Care.

Edwin Arlington Robinson (1869–1935)

Once you have found the rhetorical devices in your poem, consider their impact. In "Search for Victims" you will find a number of similes. The creeks that "brawled from their gutters like drunks" (line 5) show the shift from rainstorm to flood; the force of the river is indicated in lines 9–10: "wielding uprooted trees like battering rams." The quiet devastation left by the storm and flood is suggested by the last two lines: "tissues tossed to trees, from which they droop like Spanish moss."

Probably the "bed" that the river leaves is a literal term (rivers do have beds) rather than a personification. Check the meanings listed for "face" in an unabridged dictionary before you decide whether "Mountains lost their faces" (lines 5–6) is a personification or the use of a technical term, or both.

STEP 9

EXAMINE THE POEM CAUTIOUSLY
FOR SYMBOLS

You should be cautious in trying to identify symbols, and you should not feel compelled to invent them, because not all poems contain them. In fact, if the poet has used any, you have probably already underlined them on your worksheet as images, since symbols are essentially images with expanded meaning. In addition, the metaphors, similes, and words with multiple meanings that the poet is using may involve symbols. In general, there are two kinds of symbols, which many critics call *public* (or traditional) and *private*. Public symbols have traditional meanings, and the poet can be fairly sure that most readers will understand them. For example, a rose is a well-known symbol of love. What impact do the symbols of Christianity ("Magi," "Calvary") have on the following poem?

The Magi

Now as at all times I can see in the mind's eye,
In their stiff, painted clothes, the pale unsatisfied ones
Appear and disappear in the blue depth of the sky
With all their ancient faces like rain-beaten stones,
And all their helms of silver hovering side by side,
And all their eyes still fixed, hoping to find once more,
Being by Calvary's turbulence unsatisfied,
The uncontrollable mystery on the bestial floor.

William Butler Yeats (1865–1939)

Private symbols can mean anything the poet wishes them to, and this meaning becomes apparent only from the way they are used in the poem, as the following poem illustrates:

Domination of Black

At night, by the fire,
The colors of the bushes
And of the fallen leaves,
Repeating themselves,
Turned in the room,
Like the leaves themselves
Turning in the wind.
Yes: but the color of the heavy hemlocks
Came striding.
And I remembered the cry of the peacocks.

The colors of their tails
Were like the leaves themselves
Turning in the wind,
In the twilight wind.
They swept over the room,
Just as they flew from the boughs of the hemlocks
Down to the ground.
I heard them cry—the peacocks.
Was it a cry against the twilight
Or against the leaves themselves
Turning in the wind,
Turning as the flames
Turned in the fire,
Turning as the tails of the peacocks
Turned in the loud fire,
Loud as the hemlocks
Full of the cry of the peacocks?
Or was it a cry against the hemlocks?

Out of the window,
I saw how the planets gathered
Like the leaves themselves
Turning in the wind.
I saw how the night came,
Came striding like the color of the heavy hemlocks.

I felt afraid.
And I remembered the cry of the peacocks.

Wallace Stevens (1879–1955)

Sometimes, public and private symbols merge. In "Search for Victims," the storm, already a public symbol for disorder and upheaval in the universe, becomes also a private symbol. It represents all the hostile forces that people sense in the world, forces that seem at times to involve more than inanimate enmity.

If the symbols are not immediately obvious, chances are there are none in the poem. Many poets deliberately write poems that use only images. For example, William Carlos Williams often tried simply to instill a picture in the reader's mind, as in the following poem:

The Red Wheelbarrow

so much depends
upon

a red wheel
barrow

glazed with rain
water

beside the white
chickens.

William Carlos Williams (1883–1963)

Poets use symbols for the same reason they use images: to say something complex in a concise way. A symbol or symbols can contribute greatly to, or even sum up, the overall impact of the poem. In the poem by Stevens, the dark hemlocks and the cry of the peacocks seem to become symbolic, individually and together, of approaching death. Because literary symbols, unlike mathematical ones, have no precise, rigid meaning, readers of a poem may not always agree whether a word or a phrase is used as a symbol. In an essay expressing your response to a poem, your interpretation must be based on your own opinion, formed and supported by your careful study of the poem.

STEP **10**

WRITE YOUR PAPER

There are, of course, any number of ways to write about your response to a poem or to any other imaginative work. Six of the most basic types are (1) *analysis of a single aspect;* (2) *analysis of multiple aspects;* (3) *comparison and contrast;* (4) *exploration of a problem;* (5) *explication* of a part or of the whole; and (6) *evaluation*. While more complex papers may use a combination of more than one of these types of writing, as well as other patterns of exposition, it is generally wise to try to master the individual types or patterns before trying to combine them.

Before you begin to write a paper, consider which type or pattern of writing seems most appropriate to the expression of your response. (1) Perhaps a single aspect of the poem—say, its imagery —made an impact on you: review the notes you made under Step 7 to help you prepare a *thesis sentence,* or *topic sentence,* that indicates you are discussing a single aspect of the poem. (2) If you want to discuss more than one aspect of the poem, such as its rhyme, meter, and imagery, your thesis sentence should include all the aspects you plan to discuss, generally with a clause or phrase for each. (3) Comparison and contrast of aspects found in more than one poem require you to indicate the points of comparison in your thesis sentence. (4) You may not be able to present a firm solution to a particular problem you find with the poem: symbolism, for example, can admit of more than one interpretation. State your solution (if you have one) in your thesis sentence, and indicate the kinds of evidence you will marshal in support of your solution. (5) Explication of a poem or part of a poem involves stating the poem's theme, explaining the theme, and presenting your reasons for formulating the theme in the way you have. (6) Presenting organized arguments in support of your opinion is crucial to a paper of evaluation, which is often persuasive in nature: as with the thesis sentence for the exploration of a problem, state your opinion or evaluation in your thesis sentence, and indicate the sorts of evidence you will present. Since a carefully written thesis sentence can be a miniature outline for your paper, write it as precisely as possible in order to make the rest of your writing easier.

In the last step of each section in this book, you will find a discussion of these six types of writing with suggested techniques for using one or more of them, and two student papers that exemplify two of the types of writing. In this section we will concentrate on explication, analysis of a single aspect, and comparison and contrast.

If you decide to write an essay of *explication*, you should first try to make a brief statement of the *theme* of the poem. The statement of theme is different from the "headline" of your prose paraphrase (Step 2), because the theme of a poem is its underlying idea, whether it is explicitly stated or only implied in the poem. Deciding what the theme is will involve careful consideration of everything you have noticed in working with the poem, since each aspect you have noticed may contribute to the theme in some way. In order to state the theme, you will need to look back at your paraphrase and your worksheet notes and jot down a list of your ideas. (You might take another look at the sample worksheets on pages 5, 13–14, 14–15, and 18.) One student's statement of theme for "Search for Victims" was:

> Although nature can destroy careless, unwary humanity, it can also teach people a lesson—both about nature and about themselves—if they are willing to learn, and thus can provide hope for the future.

Now you can incorporate the poem's theme and a summary of your reasons for deciding on that theme—from your list of ideas—into the thesis statement for your paper. Often, a good way to get started is to jot down a rough thesis statement, which can then be expanded into a brief outline of points. Each part of the thesis can be thought of as a section or "box" to fill with the ideas you have already written down and with other ideas that may occur to you. Naturally, you will want to refine, or polish, your thesis statement before using it in a paper. One student's rough thesis and outline looked like this:

In this paper I want to explicate each section of Robert Grey's three-movement poem "Search for Victims," in order to show how he uses structure, meter, imagery, and symbols to develop the theme of his poem.

I. Grey's three-movement poem
   A. contrasts in images and activity
   B. use of sounds to make contrast
   C. note before-during-after view
II. Explicate each section—the images, symbols, and meter in each
III. Develop the theme
   "Search for Victims" is also hopeful search for self—increase in knowledge is lesson that people can learn through nature

Pull from your worksheet points that fit into the appropriate section of your outline, use the outline to write a rough draft of your paper, and refine your thesis statement so that it more accurately reflects the insights of your paper. For example, the student who wrote a paper on "Search for Victims" refined his thesis statement as shown on the next page.

An explication of Robert Grey's three-movement poem "Search for Victims" reveals that he has given careful attention to structure, meter, imagery, and symbols to describe the disaster nature can inflict on people who ignore its warnings and to express a hope that people can yet somehow remain open enough to nature's lesson to understand both nature and, through it, themselves.

At this point, you should test your rough draft for coherence by jotting in the margin the main idea or ideas you see in each paragraph. Often when you do this, you will see that you have repeated points or separated related points that logically belong together. If you see that you have done this, you should cut out the repetition and group the related parts together. It is a good idea to test the order of the points jotted in the margin against the order you set up in your thesis sentence, to see if you have forgotten to discuss some aspect of your thesis in your paper. Then you are ready to begin to write and polish the final draft of your paper.

Though we have been discussing only explication so far, your thesis statement must show precisely what you intend to do no matter what kind of theme you are writing. Always look back over the worksheet for your notes that relate to the particular approach you have chosen to use. For example, if you are writing a theme on only a *single aspect*—say, imagery—use the notes you made in Step 7. The questions you asked and answered there will form a sketchy outline of your paper. Here are one student's notes for Step 7 on Stevens' "Domination of Black":

Stanza 1	Visual images linked to auditory images—flames—brightly colored leaves—fall, die (*dark*) (black)—*dark* hemlocks—cry of peacocks
Stanza 2	Hint of fear—interlocking visual images with auditory—brightly colored tail—leaves in wind—fall, twilight (*dark*) (black)—cry of peacocks

> Stanza 3   Greater fear
> sight and sound unite in mind
> window view: planets—leaves in wind—night
> (*dark*) (black)—*dark* hemlocks, cry of peacocks
> fear is now terror of blackness
> death—eternity

Revise your thesis and make a rough outline; write the rough draft and refine your thesis statement. Test for coherence (as suggested above) and begin polishing your draft into the finished paper.

If you have decided to write an essay that *compares or contrasts* two poems, or a poem and a film, story, or play, the easiest way to begin is to make a chart listing the similarities or differences (or both) between the two works. For example, suppose you have decided to compare and contrast "Search for Victims" with Robert Frost's "Once by the Pacific" (page 30). Decide what points of comparison you need to consider in your essay, and list them in the left margin. Then fill in the appropriate sections across the page, using your notes, and write your rough thesis statement. On the right, say whether the poems are similar or different on each point. Your chart might look something like this:

Points of comparison	"Search for Victims"	"Once by the Pacific"	Similarity or Difference
Structure	Sonnet	Sonnet	Similarity
Subject	Storm (nature) Also aftermath	Storm-sea (nature) Ends with threat?	Similarity but also difference
Images Rhetorical devices	Sound, sight images. Most merely descriptive. One personification. Moss image implies hope.	Sight, sound images. Water personified—also night? All show nature hostile to humanity.	Both
Theme	Nature both destroyer and healer of people who heed its lesson.	Nature malevolent and hostile to humanity. Threatens not only bad night but end to human existence.	Difference

The first student paper that follows is an explication; the second is an analysis of a single aspect. You will find an example of analysis of more than one aspect in Section II on the story, an example of comparison and contrast in Section III on drama, and an exploration of a problem in Section IV on film. Evaluation is discussed in Section II, Step 9.

AN EXPLICATION OF "SEARCH FOR VICTIMS"

RANDALL CROTTS

An explication of Robert Grey's three-movement poem "Search for Victims" reveals that he has given careful attention to structure, meter, imagery, and symbols to describe the disaster nature can inflict on people who ignore its warnings and to express a hope that people can yet somehow remain open enough to nature's lesson to understand both nature and, through it, themselves.

The poem, formally a sonnet, involves three movements, which present a three-part progression. The movements contrast in visual and sound imagery and in the different kinds of activity described in order to give a before-during-after view of the subject. The onomatopoetic use of assonance and consonance lets us hear the difference between the three time periods and prepares us for the resolution of the end.

The first section ends in the fifth line, where the quiet tolerance of the typical storm ends, where familiarity ends. This section of the poem cites the experience of the storm in familiar "pops" and "creaks." The emphasis here is on assonance: the high front vowels are the sounds of the "wind in the eaves." We also hear the quick sound of raindrops on roofs. There is security in these sounds because the scene of violence is as yet unopened; there is a serenity despite the storm.

But the first statement is conditional; the deceptively simple word "until" leaves open a possibility of a counterstatement, and the second portion of the poem unfolds strong confirmation of that possibility. Beginning slowly, it displays the power with which the river tears and washes away the artifacts of human industry. The emphasis here is on harsh, hard sounds—a hard *s* next to a hard consonant, for example—so that we experience the force of the storm. The storm's violence is also conveyed through the irregular meter; and in the five consecutive heavy stresses of line 6—the height of the storm—we hear the "battering rams" of line 10 before we see them. The images of this movement are well chosen: the "boards" and "tin" that are washed away have caused the "pops" and "creaks" of the first section, thus tying the sections closely together—one is the result of the other. The river smashes, destroys, and erodes while employing the weapons of a natural force (trees). "Creaks" are washed away in "creeks."

The break between the second and third sections occurs in the line that breaks the poem into two stanzas. There is no slow movement of one section into the other, as there is between the first two; instead the line is clearly drawn between two kinds of description, so the physical distance between the two on the page is appropriate to the subject as well as to the sonnet form.

The third section, in which the storm has passed, is optimistic about repairing and restoring the community as it describes the search for bodies and for "knowledge." Sounds here are soft, except for the harsh *sk* sound in "scars," the first visual image of the section. Yet the scars will heal, we realize with the "townsmen," if the lesson of the storm has been learned. The only other visual images in the section combine in the human tissues—Spanish moss simile. At first this double image seems out of place in a stanza evaluating the devastation as contrasted to the emphasis on vivid images in the preceding stanzas. It is here, however, that the theme of the poem begins to emerge through a close study of possible different interpretations of the last five lines. Making these interpretations requires playing with punctuation in order to reveal unexpected meanings. Look, for instance, at the beginning of the last part of the poem:

> There will be time to live
> when scars heal, time for townsmen to increase
> their knowledge, if their flesh is sensitive:
> they search, below flood-exhumed tissues tossed
> to trees, from which they droop like Spanish moss.

The first line quoted here seems to be an important statement in itself; the word "live" concluding the first line of the stanza states unequivocally that life prevails. Then, reading the three lines as a unit (ending with "sensitive") leads to an interpretation that people will learn only if they are sensitive to nature. For in the next line (passing over the commas and ending the thought with "tissues"), the statement could be interpreted as describing a search beneath the body from which the spirit of life has been "flood-exhumed," or, in other words, a look beyond the physical to the qualities of nature, which are oblivious to any special position or condition of humanity. For people are "tossed to trees" in the violence preceding, victims of the "battering rams" of nature. In the final image, the bodies—that is, the physical—hang limp and empty, lifeless and crushed "like Spanish moss," overcome by the force of raging, misunderstood, misinterpreted, unwatched nature. Yet since the Spanish moss is living, though it resembles something lifeless, there is a final paradoxical affirmation of life in the presence of death.

So the "search for victims" is not only the search for the bodies of the dead, but a search for the self that can be found only in nature. The continuity and symbolism of the first two sections become obvious. The warnings of nature, unheeded, do indeed bring disaster; yet people must renew themselves in nature and start again to "live when scars heal," when "knowledge" is regained and "mountains" regain their "faces." So, finally, the flood of devastation becomes more than the water; it is the omnipotence and enduring manifestation of nature symbolically washing itself clean.

The last line of the poem is in perfect iambic pentameter.

The striking contrast of this line to the irregular meter of the storm passage resolves in the wake of the storm both the tension between form and content and the paradox of life in the midst of death.

IMAGERY IN "DOMINATION OF BLACK"

GLORIA MC GETTIGAN

In "Domination of Black," [1] Wallace Stevens encounters the fear produced by the ideas of death and eternity. Stevens does not feel terror as an emotional, romantic outpouring of feeling; instead, the fear is an intellectual experience that is brought to fruition by his imagination and a remembered cry of peacocks. The poem's effectiveness is increased by the suggestive qualities of the images, which underscore its emotional power.

"Domination of Black" can be paraphrased as follows: a man is sitting at night in front of a fire. While he watches the flickering flames, he is reminded of the bright colors of the fallen autumn leaves; however, fallen leaves die and the darkness of the hemlocks brings to his memory the discordant cry of the peacocks.

In the second stanza, the brilliant colors of the peacock's tail remind him of the colors of the leaves turning in the wind. The wind becomes a twilight wind, and the cry of the peacock repeats itself. The man's terror increases as he questions why the peacock cries. What was the cry against? Was it the approaching twilight, the fallen leaves, or the hemlocks whose shape became more ominous as the darkness approached?

In the third stanza, the man looks out the window at "the planets gathered" turning like the fallen leaves in the wind.

[1] All references in my paper are to the reprinting of "Domination of Black" found on page 35 of this volume, unless otherwise noted. [See also the Documentation Checklist on pages 185–87.]

The blackness of night comes. It is as imposing as the heavy hemlocks, and he once more remembers the cry of the peacocks. He is afraid because he realizes that color and movement, which give richness and life to the physical world, must yield to the darkness, just as the autumn leaves fall from the trees and lose their color.

The title is important in setting the mood for the build-up of terror that is found in the poem. The connotation of the word "domination" eliminates any feeling of freedom or of choice. To be dominated means to be ruled, controlled, or governed by something, in this case, by black. The definition of the color black produces an interesting image. "Black is the darkest of all colors. In the theory of color, white is produced by all the colors in light mixed in the proportion in which they are found in the rainbow. The absorption of all the colors found in light produces black. Black is really the absence of color." [2] Black is also symbolic of death and unpleasantness, as in "black despair" and "black looks." We can, therefore, see in the title the frightening domination of black that can reduce life to nothing by absorbing all the richness of color.

This image is further developed throughout the poem. In the first stanza, the black of night is dispelled by the brightness of the fire. The man is reminded of the colors of bushes and fallen leaves that are turning in the wind. Blackness intrudes and enters the room in the dark green color of the hemlocks, which grows darker as the night approaches. Stevens personifies the color of the heavy hemlocks that "came striding" into the room. The tension is increased by the image aroused by the use of the verb "striding." In the personification of the color of the hemlock there is a vigor, an arrogance, that intrudes upon a pleasant scene and frightens.

In the second stanza, the wind becomes a "twilight wind" (line 14) and, in turn, becomes a threatening wind. The colors of the leaves and of the peacocks' tails turn in the wind, but eventually the twilight wind brings the leaves to

[2] "Black," *The World Book Encyclopedia*, 1966, B-2, p. 304.

the ground for their final rest and drops the peacocks from the hemlock boughs.

In the third stanza, the man looks out the window and sees the "planets gathered." Their whiteness, produced by a mixture of all the colors in the rainbow, is not strong enough to dispel the blackness of night, which Stevens again personifies with the verbal phrase "came striding like the color of the heavy hemlocks" (line 34). The blackness is more dominant than the light of life. The planets turn like the leaves in the wind, but they are a fragile image in comparison to the "striding night" and "heavy hemlocks." The color of the night seems to threaten the existence of the planets in the universe and to cause the poet's fear and the peacock's cry. Stevens has now in an act of the mind taken the blackness out of the confines of the room and applied its presence and power to the whole world.

The fear that is produced by the color black, by the color of the hemlocks, by the twilight wind, and by the night is emotionally heightened by the repetitive use of the memory of the cry of the peacocks. The peacock is a richly colored bird that is treasured for its beauty. It is in sharp contrast to the lack of color that blackness holds. The peacock's cry is sometimes described as a raucous, wailing, discordant shriek, and it is said to occur before a disaster. The poet remembers the cry of the peacocks in the first stanza when the color of the heavy hemlock strides into the room. He questions the reason for the cry in the second stanza. In the third stanza the poet's fear and the cry of the peacocks are united in a joint response to the blackness of night.

SUGGESTIONS FOR WRITING

I. Papers on one aspect of a work:
   1. Allusion in "Helen" (see Step 3)
   2. Double meaning in "The Hand That Signed the Paper Felled a City" (Step 3)

IV. Papers exploring a problem:
   1. Is "Search for Victims" a sonnet?
   2. What is the function of the stanzas in "Get Up and Bar the Door"?
   3. Are the references to "fire" and "ice" in Frost's poem "Fire and Ice" literal, or do they shade into symbol?
 V. Papers of explication:
   1. Explicate Sidney's poem from *Astrophel and Stella.*
   2. Explicate "Memories of an Early Marriage."
   3. Choose a poem you like and explicate your response to it.
VI. Papers of evaluation: Choose any poem you are studying and evaluate it. (Be careful to base your judgments on what the poem itself says, not on what you think it should say.)

Section II
Analyzing and Writing About a
STORY

In a short story, a writer has more room than in a poem, and less than in a novel or play, to create a situation, present a conflict, develop a character. Close reading and careful analysis of different aspects of a story, as suggested by the steps discussed in this section, should help you to explore your response to a story and to choose ways to record it.

STEP 1

READ THE STORY CAREFULLY

As you read the story you have chosen, you will be making notes for yourself on a worksheet, or in the margins if the book is your own. On the following page is a retelling by British author W. Somerset Maugham of a very old tale: begin to practice your analytic techniques with this story.

APPOINTMENT IN SAMARRA

W. SOMERSET MAUGHAM (1874–1965)

Death speaks: There was a merchant in Bagdad who sent his servant to market to buy provisions and in a little while the servant came back, white and trembling, and said, Master, just now when I was in the market-place I was jostled by a woman in the crowd and when I turned I saw it was Death that jostled me. She looked at me and made a threatening gesture; now, lend me your horse, and I will ride away from this city and avoid my fate. I will go to Samarra and there Death will not find me. The merchant lent him his horse, and the servant mounted it, and he dug his spurs in its flanks and as fast as the horse could gallop he went. Then the merchant went down to the market-place and he saw me standing in the crowd and he came to me and said, Why did you make a threatening gesture to my servant when you saw him this morning? That was not a threatening gesture, I said, it was only a start of surprise. I was astonished to see him in Bagdad, for I had an appointment with him tonight in Samarra.

STEP 2

DECIDE WHAT THE STORY IS ABOUT

After you have read a story, ask yourself if it created in you a particular mood or impression, such as fear, compassion, or bewilderment. Perhaps the story made another kind of impression on you. Think of a word or two—probably a noun—that names this mood, emotion, or impression. Then try to be more specific: qualify your noun with an adjective or two. This should result in a phrase that characterizes the story for you; underline the key words in that phrase. Think of the phrase as a title or headline for your next step: a brief summary of the story. Try to keep your brief summary in the same tense as the story. One student worksheet for the tale you have just read looked like this:

> Death—inescapable
> The inescapability of Death
> Death tells the tale to a merchant—
> A servant, having seen Death at a Baghdad market, borrowed his master's horse and fled to Samarra—where, though he could not have known it, he had his real appointment with Death.

Look at the title of the story: does it relate either to your summary or to your statement of emotion? Or do you think the title refers to something else about the story? If you think the title has some significance, add a brief phrase about it to your worksheet. For example, the word "appointment" has connotations of inescapability. (You might wish to read the novel *Appointment in Samarra*, by John O'Hara, in which this tale is reprinted facing the title page.)

STEP 3
ANALYZE THE POINT OF VIEW

When you read a story, it is through someone else's eyes—from someone else's *point of view*—that you view the setting, see the action, observe the characters, and hear the conversations. Depending on the powers the author has granted to the *narrator*, or teller of the tale, you may even get inside a character's mind and learn what he or she thinks and feels. In the *first person* point of view,

"I" and "we" are used; in the *third person* point of view, "he," "she," and "they" are used. Sometimes the narrator is *omniscient,* knowing what all the characters do and possibly what they think and feel. Or, in the *limited third person* point of view, other characters or events are reported only as they appear to one particular character, called a *central intelligence.* There are many variations on these basic types of point of view, sometimes within the same story. Perhaps this outline will help you:

I. First person point of view
    A. Narrator is participant
    B. Narrator is observer
II. Third person point of view
    A. Narrator is *omniscient*—knows everything
        1. Editorial—includes narrator's comments on situations
        2. Objective—narrator merely reports situations
    B. Reader's knowledge is *limited*—confined to that of a central intelligence, a particular character

Decide on the point of view of your story, and write it on your worksheet. If the point of view shifts within the story, or if some special effect is created, jot this down too. Do you feel that you are a fly on the wall, seeing and hearing everything? Have you been given access to all the thoughts of one or more characters?

Point of view, in addition to admitting the reader into the story, can sometimes have other uses. It can encourage the reader to identify with a character or a situation. Certainly, if we can see a character's actions and thoughts, we can gain insight into his or her feelings and motives. Does the point of view in the story you are reading have any particular use? Make a note about this on your worksheet.

In your notes, be careful not to identify the *narrator* of the story with the *author.* Remember, you are reading fiction, not autobiography; for example, many of Edgar Allan Poe's short stories are in the first person, yet you know that all the adventures did not happen to Poe himself. The narrator is a character created by the author to tell the tale; the narrator is sometimes called the *persona,* especially when the narrator is merely an observer, not a participant in the story.

Consider, as specifically as possible, the various changes that would have to be made if the story were to be presented from another point of view. Do not just say, "It wouldn't be the same"; list a few aspects that would have to change. Persons on different corners of an intersection could view the same traffic accident very differently, and their accounts of it might not agree with those of the drivers involved. In Maugham's tale, Death is the narrator, quoting the servant in the first part and using "I" in response to the merchant's question. Death reports all the actions and words. The servant does not know that he will meet Death "tonight in Samarra"; since he has fled Baghdad, he has no way of knowing that his master meets and converses with Death, nor can he hear Death's response.

STEP 4

ANALYZE THE SETTING

The place and time in which a story occurs form its *setting.* Decide approximately when the events in your story might have happened. Does the story take place in a specified time and place, such as Renaissance Italy or present-day America? Perhaps the time is unspecified, and the story is therefore applicable to any period, as in "Appointment in Samarra." Time may shift within a story; look for *flashbacks* to earlier action, which may provide you with extra information about a situation or a character's motives. Make notes on your worksheet about the times and places in your story, noting when and how they influence a character or an action.

Look at the story to see whether the setting is fully described or only suggested. The setting may merely provide a background for the action, but often the setting is an important part of the story. It can create a miniature world in which the characters function in a believable manner; perhaps the characters struggle against the setting or are changed by it. Note on your worksheet any comments you have about the setting and its role in the story you are analyzing.

In the following short story, a large French window is an important part of the setting.

THE OPEN WINDOW

SAKI (H. H. MUNRO) (1870–1916)

"My aunt will be down presently, Mr. Nuttel," said a very self-possessed young lady of fifteen; "in the meantime you must try and put up with me."

Framton Nuttel endeavoured to say the correct something which should duly flatter the niece of the moment without unduly discounting the aunt that was to come. Privately he doubted more than ever whether these formal visits on a succession of total strangers would do much towards helping the nerve cure which he was supposed to be undergoing.

"I know how it will be," his sister had said when he was preparing to migrate to this rural retreat; "you will bury yourself down there and not speak to a living soul, and your nerves will be worse than ever from moping. I shall just give you letters of introduction to all the people I know there. Some of them, as far as I can remember, were quite nice."

Framton wondered whether Mrs. Sappleton, the lady to whom he was presenting one of the letters of introduction, came into the nice division.

"Do you know many of the people round here?" asked the niece, when she judged that they had had sufficient silent communion.

"Hardly a soul," said Framton. "My sister was staying here, at the rectory, you know, some four years ago, and she gave me letters of introduction to some of the people here."

He made the last statement in a tone of distinct regret.

"Then you know practically nothing about my aunt?" pursued the self-possessed young lady.

"Only her name and address," admitted the caller. He was wondering whether Mrs. Sappleton was in the married or widowed state. An undefinable something about the room seemed to suggest masculine habitation.

"Her great tragedy happened just three years ago," said the child; "that would be since your sister's time."

"Her tragedy?" asked Framton; somehow in this restful country spot tragedies seemed out of place.

"You may wonder why we keep that window wide open on an October afternoon," said the niece, indicating a large French window that opened on to a lawn.

"It is quite warm for the time of the year," said Framton; "but has that window got anything to do with the tragedy?"

"Out through that window, three years ago to a day, her husband and her two young brothers went off for their day's shooting. They never came back. In crossing the moor to their favourite snipe-shooting ground they were all three engulfed in a treacherous piece of bog. It had been that dreadful wet summer, you know, and places that were safe in other years gave way suddenly without warning. Their bodies were never recovered. That was the dreadful part of it." Here the child's voice lost its self-possessed note and became falteringly human. "Poor aunt always thinks that they will come back some day, they and the little brown spaniel that was lost with them, and walk in at that window just as they used to do. That is why the window is kept open every evening till it is quite dusk. Poor dear aunt, she has often told me how they went out, her husband with his white waterproof coat over his arm, and Ronnie, her youngest brother, singing, 'Bertie, why do you bound?' as he always did to tease her, because she said it got on her nerves. Do you know, sometimes on still, quiet evenings like this, I almost get a creepy feeling that they will all walk in through that window—"

She broke off with a little shudder. It was a relief to Framton when the aunt bustled into the room with a whirl of apologies for being late in making her appearance.

"I hope Vera has been amusing you?" she said.

"She has been very interesting," said Framton.

"I hope you don't mind the open window," said Mrs. Sappleton briskly; "my husband and brothers will be home directly from shooting, and they always come in this way. They've been out for snipe in the marshes today, so they'll make a fine mess over my poor carpets. So like you men-folk, isn't it?"

She rattled on cheerfully about the shooting and the scarcity of birds, and the prospects for duck in the winter. To Framton it was all purely horrible. He made a desperate but only partially successful effort to turn the talk on to a less ghastly topic; he was conscious that his hostess was giving him only a fragment of her attention, and her eyes were constantly straying past him to the open window and the lawn beyond. It was certainly an unfortunate coincidence that he should have paid his visit on this tragic anniversary.

"The doctors agree in ordering me complete rest, an absence of mental excitement, and avoidance of anything in the nature of violent physical exercise," announced Framton, who laboured under the tolerably wide-spread delusion that total strangers and chance acquaintances are hungry for the least detail of one's ailments and infirmities, their cause and cure. "On the matter of diet they are not so much in agreement," he continued.

"No?" said Mrs. Sappleton, in a voice which only replaced a yawn at the last moment. Then she suddenly brightened into alert attention—but not to what Framton was saying.

"Here they are at last!" she cried. "Just in time for tea, and don't they look as if they were muddy up to the eyes!"

Framton shivered slightly and turned towards the niece with a look intended to convey sympathetic comprehension. The child was staring out through the open window with dazed horror in her eyes. In a chill shock of nameless fear Framton swung round in his seat and looked in the same direction.

In the deepening twilight three figures were walking across the lawn towards the window; they all carried guns under their arms, and one of them was additionally burdened with a white coat hung over his shoulders. A tired brown spaniel kept close at their heels. Noiselessly they neared the house, and then a hoarse young voice chanted out of the dusk: "I said, Bertie, why do you bound?"

Framton grabbed wildly at his stick and hat; the hall-door, the gravel-drive, and the front gate were dimly noted stages in his headlong retreat. A cyclist coming along the road had to run into the hedge to avoid imminent collision.

"Here we are, my dear," said the bearer of the white mackintosh, coming in through the window; "fairly muddy, but most of it's dry. Who was that who bolted out as we came up?"

"A most extraordinary man, a Mr. Nuttel," said Mrs. Sappleton; "could only talk about his illnesses, and dashed off without a word of good-bye or apology when you arrived. One would think he had seen a ghost."

"I expect it was the spaniel," said the niece calmly; "he told me he had a horror of dogs. He was once hunted into a cemetery somewhere on the banks of the Ganges by a pack of pariah dogs, and had to spend the night in a newly dug grave with the creatures snarling and grinning and foaming just above him. Enough to make any one lose their nerve."

Romance at short notice was her speciality.

STEP 5

ANALYZE THE CHARACTERS

A story usually involves characters, some of whom are more important than others. On your worksheet, make a list in which you group the characters according to their importance in the story. Underline the name of the major character, the *protagonist*. You might wish to make two columns, one for more important and one for less important characters.

Look at your list of important characters. Is their physical appearance described? How detailed are these descriptions, and who gives them to you—the narrator or another character? Can you identify the characters by what they say or how they say it? Do their actions characterize them? Write a brief phrase to identify each major character beside his or her name; for example, you would almost surely put "nervous" beside Framton Nuttel's name. Do the same for your column of minor characters if you have made one.

How fully developed are the characters, especially the protagonist? Are their actions *believable,* motivated in a way you can understand? If some characters are more fully developed than others, make a note of it. E. M. Forster's terms *flat* and *round* might apply to one or more characters in your story: a flat character has only one dimension or identifying characteristic, while a round character is more complex, more fully developed. Perhaps the terms *static* and *dynamic* would be more suitable to describe the characters in your story: things may happen to static characters, but they remain unchanged; dynamic characters undergo change or growth. A story is not necessarily bad if it includes a number of flat or static characters, or good if all its characters are round or dynamic. Decide, too, whether any of the characters represent certain attitudes or ideas, or are drawn even more broadly, so that they become *stereotypes,* such as the potbellied bigot, the crafty fox, the strong and silent lawman.

ANALYZE THE PLOT

A story involves characters who are in a *situation*. Usually, the situation changes in some way—called the *complication*—and we see the reactions of the characters to this change. If the story is very dramatic, the complication will often set up a *conflict* between two characters. The action leading up to the turning point—to the *climax,* or *crisis*—can be called the *rising action;* the action after the turning point can be called the *falling action*. Our desire to discover how the characters react to the changed situation or to the conflict is one of the aspects of *suspense*. Notice that in considering these matters, you are looking at the "why" behind the action: you are looking at the *plot development,* or *structure,* of the story.

Plot and character are often interwoven. A decision by a character may be the turning point of the action. Or an event may cause a character to react in new ways, to grow and change. The end result of such a change, the outcome of the plot, can be called the *resolution*. Not all stories have a resolution, but the ending of every story should be compatible with the original situation; in "The Open Window," for example, Framton's hasty exit is believable, since we know that he is recuperating from a nervous disorder. Note on your worksheet whether or not this is true of your story. Does the resolution of your story require you to add any comments to your phrase identifying the main character, or to your summary?

Look a little more closely at the plot, watching for ways in which the author creates suspense. Does the dialogue or narrative contain hints of what will happen? Perhaps clues are given you by the description of the setting or of the characters. (In stories in which the protagonist approaches the ivy-covered door of an isolated mansion on the night of a full moon, there is frequently something hidden in the basement.) The technique of giving such hints is called *foreshadowing*. Perhaps the author uses *surprise* or *irony,* particularly in the falling action. "The Open Window" certainly illustrates surprise; review the story for its plot and structure.

STEP 7

ANALYZE THE IMAGERY
AND RHETORICAL DEVICES

Imagery can be used to describe the setting or the physical appearance of a character, and it can also be used in conversations to give information about either the speaker or the subject. Since imagery is the use of words or phrases that appeal to one or more of the senses, do not forget to look for images that appeal to senses other than sight. Note where you find imagery to be important, and to which sense it appeals. Does its appeal shift from one sense to another? Does it set a tone, establish a mood, present a character in a new light? For example, in "The Open Window," many readers remember vividly the scene with the returning hunter's white coat against the dusky lawn, and the hoarse voice singing.

Look carefully at the way the images are presented. Often, an author will use imagery to make comparisons, especially the direct comparison, or *simile,* and the slightly more subtle *metaphor.* (You might review these terms in the discussion of rhetorical devices in Section I, Step 8.) Notice whether particular kinds of comparisons are being made. If a character's long teeth, pointed ears, and general hairiness are mentioned every time he is described, we are bound to draw certain conclusions about what it is that he is being compared to.

Review your notes on the story. If you are still having difficulty understanding it, you may be having problems with ambiguous punctuation, unusual sentence structure, or unfamiliar words or allusions; you can glance back at Section I, Step 3, for assistance.

STEP 8

EXAMINE THE STORY CAUTIOUSLY
FOR SYMBOLS

We discussed *symbol* briefly in Step 9 of the Poetry section (and you might wish to review that discussion); one warning bears reinforcing. If you have to search desperately for a symbol, it probably is not there. And if you can pin down a precise meaning for what you see as a symbol, it is more likely to be a metaphor, since symbols extend beyond a one-to-one comparison. Readers of a story may not always agree on whether or not a particular word or phrase is used as a symbol. Be sure to back up your opinion with evidence from your careful reading of the story. In the following short fable by James Thurber, readers often discuss whether the rabbits' dilemma is symbolic of larger human problems. In the story by Eudora Welty, the main character's goal is to complete a journey; you might enjoy deciding whether the motif of a journey is symbolic.

THE RABBITS WHO CAUSED
ALL THE TROUBLE

JAMES THURBER (1894–1961)

Within the memory of the youngest child there was a family of rabbits who lived near a pack of wolves. The wolves announced that they did not like the way the rabbits were living. (The wolves were crazy about the way they themselves were living, because it was the only way to live.) One night several wolves were killed in an earthquake and this was blamed on the rabbits, for it is well known that rabbits pound on the ground with their hind legs and cause earthquakes. On another night one of the wolves was killed by a bolt of lightning and this was also blamed on the rabbits, for it is well known that lettuce-eaters cause lightning. The wolves threatened to civilize the rabbits if they didn't behave, and the rabbits decided to run away to a desert island. But the other animals, who lived at a great distance, shamed them, saying, "You must stay where you are and be brave. This is no world for escapists. If the wolves attack you, we will come to your aid, in all probability." So the rabbits continued to live near the wolves and one day there was a terrible flood which drowned a great many wolves. This was blamed on the rabbits, for it is well known that carrot-nibblers with long ears cause floods. The wolves descended on the rabbits, for their own good, and imprisoned them in a dark cave, for their own protection.

When nothing was heard about the rabbits for some weeks, the other animals demanded to know what had happened to them. The wolves replied that the rabbits had been eaten and since they had been eaten the affair was a purely internal matter. But the other animals warned that they might possibly unite against the wolves unless some reason was given for the destruction of the rabbits. So the wolves gave them one. "They were trying to escape," said the wolves, "and, as you know, this is no world for escapists."

Moral: Run, don't walk, to the nearest desert island.

A WORN PATH

EUDORA WELTY (1909–   )

It was December—a bright frozen day in the early morning. Far out in the country there was an old Negro woman with her head tied in a red rag, coming along a path through the pinewoods. Her name was Phoenix Jackson. She was very old and small and she walked slowly in the dark pine shadows, moving a little from side to side in her steps, with the balanced heaviness and lightness of a pendulum in a grandfather clock. She carried a thin, small cane made from an umbrella, and with this she kept tapping the frozen earth in front of her. This made a grave and persistent noise in the still air, that seemed meditative like the chirping of a solitary little bird.

She wore a dark striped dress reaching down to her shoe tops, and an equally long apron of bleached sugar sacks, with a full pocket: all neat and tidy, but every time she took a step she might have fallen over her shoelaces, which dragged from her unlaced shoes. She looked straight ahead. Her eyes were blue with age. Her skin had a pattern all its own of numberless branching wrinkles and as though a whole little tree stood in the middle of her forehead, but a golden color ran underneath, and the two knobs of her cheeks were illumined by a yellow burning under the dark. Under the red rag her hair came down on her neck in the frailest of ringlets, still black, and with an odor like copper.

Now and then there was a quivering in the thicket. Old Phoenix said, "Out of my way, all you foxes, owls, beetles, jack rabbits, coons and wild animals! . . . Keep out from under these feet, little bob-whites. . . . Keep the big wild hogs out of my path. Don't let none of those come running my direction. I got a long way." Under her small black-freckled hand her cane, limber as a buggy whip, would switch at the brush as if to rouse up any hiding things.

On she went. The woods were deep and still. The sun made the pine needles almost too bright to look at, up where the wind rocked. The cones dropped as light as feathers. Down in the hollow was the mourning dove—it was not too late for him.

The path ran up a hill. "Seem like there is chains about my feet, time I get this far," she said, in the voice of argument old people keep to use with themselves. "Something always take a hold of me on this hill—pleads I should stay."

After she got to the top she turned and gave a full, severe look behind her where she had come. "Up through pines," she said at length. "Now down through oaks."

Her eyes opened their widest, and she started down gently. But before she got to the bottom of the hill a bush caught her dress.

Her fingers were busy and intent, but her skirts were full and long, so that before she could pull them free in one place they were caught in another. It was not possible to allow the dress to tear. "I in the thorny bush," she said. "Thorns, you doing your appointed work. Never want to let folks pass, no sir. Old eyes thought you was a pretty little *green* bush."

Finally, trembling all over, she stood free, and after a moment dared to stoop for her cane.

"Sun so high!" she cried, leaning back and looking, while the thick tears went over her eyes. "The time getting all gone here."

At the foot of this hill was a place where a log was laid across the creek.

"Now comes the trial," said Phoenix.

Putting her right foot out, she mounted the log and shut her eyes. Lifting her skirt, leveling her cane fiercely before her, like a festival figure in some parade, she began to march across. Then she opened her eyes and she was safe on the other side.

"I wasn't as old as I thought," she said.

But she sat down to rest. She spread her skirts on the bank around her and folded her hands over her knees. Up above her was a tree in a pearly cloud of mistletoe. She did not dare to close her eyes, and when a little boy brought her a plate with a slice of marble-cake on it she spoke to him. "That would be acceptable," she said. But when she went to take it there was just her own hand in the air.

So she left that tree, and had to go through a barbed-wire fence. There she had to creep and crawl, spreading her knees and stretching her fingers like a baby trying to climb the steps. But she talked loudly to herself: she could not let her dress be torn now, so late in the day, and she could not pay for having her arm or her leg sawed off if she got caught fast where she was.

At last she was safe through the fence and risen up out in the clearing. Big dead trees, like black men with one arm, were standing in the purple stalks of the withered cotton field. There sat a buzzard.

"Who you watching?"

In the furrow she made her way along.

"Glad this not the season for bulls," she said, looking sideways, "and the good Lord made his snakes to curl up and sleep in the winter. A pleasure I don't see no two-headed snake coming around that tree, where it come once. It took a while to get by him, back in the summer."

She passed through the old cotton and went into a field of dead corn. It whispered and shook and was taller than her head. "Through the maze now," she said, for there was no path.

Then there was something tall, black, and skinny there, moving before her.

At first she took it for a man. It could have been a man dancing in the field. But she stood still and listened, and it did not make a sound. It was as silent as a ghost.

"Ghost," she said sharply, "who be you the ghost of? For I have heard of nary death close by."

But there was no answer—only the ragged dancing in the wind.

She shut her eyes, reached out her hand, and touched a sleeve. She found a coat and inside that an emptiness, cold as ice.

"You scarecrow," she said. Her face lighted. "I ought to be shut up for good," she said with laughter. "My senses is gone. I too old. I the oldest people I ever know. Dance, old scarecrow," she said, "while I dancing with you."

She kicked her foot over the furrow, and with mouth drawn down, shook her head once or twice in a little strutting way. Some husks blew down and whirled in streamers about her skirts.

Then she went on, parting her way from side to side with the cane, through the whispering field. At last she came to the end, to a wagon track where the silver grass blew between the red ruts. The quail were walking around like pullets, seeming all dainty and unseen.

"Walk pretty," she said. "This the easy place. This the easy going."

She followed the track, swaying through the quiet bare fields, through the little strings of trees silver in their dead leaves, past cabins silver from weather, with the doors and windows boarded shut, all like old women under a spell sitting there. "I walking in their sleep," she said, nodding her head vigorously.

In a ravine she went where a spring was silently flowing through a hollow log. Old Phoenix bent and drank. "Sweet-gum makes the water sweet," she said, and drank more. "Nobody know who made this well, for it was here when I was born."

The track crossed a swampy part where the moss hung as white as lace from every limb. "Sleep on, alligators, and blow your bubbles." Then the track went into the road.

Deep, deep the road went down between the high green-colored banks. Overhead the live-oaks met, and it was as dark as a cave.

A black dog with a lolling tongue came up out of the weeds by the ditch. She was meditating, and not ready, and when he came at her she only hit him a little with her cane. Over she went in the ditch, like a little puff of milkweed.

Down there, her senses drifted away. A dream visited her, and she reached her hand up, but nothing reached down and gave her a pull. So she lay there and presently went to talking. "Old woman," she said to herself, "that black dog come up out of the weeds to stall you off, and now there he sitting on his fine tail, smiling at you."

A white man finally came along and found her—a hunter, a young man, with his dog on a chain.

"Well, Granny!" he laughed. "What are you doing there?"

"Lying on my back like a June-bug waiting to be turned over, mister," she said, reaching up her hand.

He lifted her up, gave her a swing in the air, and set her down. "Anything broken, Granny?"

"No sir, them old dead weeds is springy enough," said Phoenix, when she had got her breath. "I thank you for your trouble."

"Where do you live, Granny?" he asked, while the two dogs were growling at each other.

"Away back yonder, sir, behind the ridge. You can't even see it from here."

"On your way home?"

"No sir, I going to town."

"Why, that's too far! That's as far as I walk when I come out myself, and I get something for my trouble." He patted the stuffed bag he carried, and there hung down a little closed claw. It was one of the bob-whites, with its beak hooked bitterly to show it was dead. "Now you go on home, Granny!"

"I bound to go to town, mister," said Phoenix. "The time come around."

He gave another laugh, filling the whole landscape. "I know you old colored people! Wouldn't miss going to town to see Santa Claus!"

But something held old Phoenix very still. The deep lines in her face went into a fierce and different radiation. Without warning, she had seen with her own eyes a flashing nickel fall out of the man's pocket onto the ground.

"How old are you, Granny?" he was saying.

"There is no telling, mister," she said, "no telling."

Then she gave a little cry and clapped her hands and said, "Git on away from here, dog! Look! Look at that dog!" She laughed as if in admiration. "He ain't scared of nobody. He a big black dog." She whispered, "Sic him!"

"Watch me get rid of that cur," said the man. "Sic him, Pete! Sic him!"

Phoenix heard the dogs fighting, and heard the man running and throwing sticks. She even heard a gunshot. But she was slowly bending forward by that time, further and further forward, the lids stretched down over her eyes, as if she were doing this in her sleep. Her chin was lowered almost to her knees. The yellow palm of her hand came out from the fold of her apron. Her fingers slid down and along the ground under the piece of money with the grace and care they would have in lifting an egg from under a setting hen. Then she slowly straightened up, she stood erect, and the nickel was in her apron pocket. A bird flew by. Her lips moved. "God watching me the whole time. I come to stealing."

The man came back, and his own dog panted about them. "Well, I scared him off that time," he said, and then he laughed and lifted his gun and pointed it at Phoenix.

She stood straight and faced him.

"Doesn't the gun scare you?" he said, still pointing it.

"No, sir, I seen plenty go off closer by, in my day, and for less than what I done," she said, holding utterly still.

He smiled, and shouldered the gun. "Well, Granny," he said, "you must be a hundred years old, and scared of nothing. I'd give you a dime if I had any money with me. But you take my advice and stay home, and nothing will happen to you."

"I bound to go on my way, mister," said Phoenix. She inclined her head in the red rag. Then they went in different directions, but she could hear the gun shooting again and again over the hill.

She walked on. The shadows hung from the oak trees to the road like curtains. Then she smelled wood-smoke, and smelled the river, and she saw a steeple and the cabins on their steep steps. Dozens of little black children whirled around her. There ahead was Natchez shining. Bells were ringing. She walked on.

In the paved city it was Christmas time. There were red and green electric lights strung and crisscrossed everywhere, and all turned on in the daytime. Old Phoenix would have been lost if she had not distrusted her eyesight and depended on her feet to know where to take her.

She paused quietly on the sidewalk where people were passing by. A lady came along in the crowd, carrying an armful of red-, green- and silver-wrapped presents; she gave off perfume like the red roses in hot summer, and Phoenix stopped her.

"Please, missy, will you lace up my shoe?" She held up her foot.

"What do you want, Grandma?"

"See my shoe," said Phoenix. "Do all right for out in the country, but wouldn't look right to go in a big building."

"Stand still then, Grandma," said the lady. She put her packages down on the sidewalk beside her and laced and tied both shoes tightly.

"Can't lace 'em with a cane," said Phoenix. "Thank you, missy. I doesn't mind asking a nice lady to tie up my shoe, when I gets out on the street."

Moving slowly and from side to side, she went into the big building, and into a tower of steps, where she walked up and around and around until her feet knew to stop.

She entered a door, and there she saw nailed up on the wall the document that had been stamped with the gold seal and framed in the gold frame, which matched the dream that was hung up in her head.

"Here I be," she said. There was a fixed and ceremonial stiffness over her body.

"A charity case, I suppose," said an attendant who sat at the desk before her.

But Phoenix only looked above her head. There was sweat on her face, the wrinkles in her skin shone like a bright net.

"Speak up, Grandma," the woman said. "What's your name? We must have your history, you know. Have you been here before? What seems to be the trouble with you?"

Old Phoenix only gave a twitch to her face as if a fly were bothering her.

"Are you deaf?" cried the attendant.

But then the nurse came in.

"Oh, that's just old Aunt Phoenix," she said. "She doesn't come for herself—she has a little grandson. She makes these trips just as regular as clockwork. She lives away back off the Old Natchez Trace." She bent down. "Well, Aunt Phoenix, why don't you just take a seat? We won't keep you standing after your long trip." She pointed.

The old woman sat down, bolt upright in the chair.

"Now, how is the boy?" asked the nurse.

Old Phoenix did not speak.

"I said, how is the boy?"

But Phoenix only waited and stared straight ahead, her face very solemn and withdrawn into rigidity.

"Is his throat any better?" asked the nurse. "Aunt Phoenix, don't you hear me? Is your grandson's throat any better since the last time you came for the medicine?"

With her hands on her knees, the old woman waited, silent, erect and motionless, just as if she were in armor.

"You mustn't take up our time this way, Aunt Phoenix," the nurse said. "Tell us quickly about your grandson, and get it over. He isn't dead, is he?"

At last there came a flicker and then a flame of comprehension across her face, and she spoke.

"My grandson. It was my memory had left me. There I sat and forgot why I made my long trip."

"Forgot?" The nurse frowned. "After you came so far?"

Then Phoenix was like an old woman begging a dignified forgiveness for waking up frightened in the night. "I never did go to school, I was too old at the Surrender," she said in a soft voice. "I'm an old woman without an education. It was my memory fail me. My little grandson, he is just the same, and I forgot it in the coming."

"Throat never heals, does it?" said the nurse, speaking in a loud, sure voice to old Phoenix. By now she had a card with something written on it, a little list. "Yes. Swallowed lye. When was it?— January—two-three years ago—"

Phoenix spoke unasked now. "No, missy, he not dead, he just the same. Every little while his throat begin to close up again, and he not able to swallow. He not get his breath. He not able to help himself. So the time come around, and I go on another trip for the soothing medicine."

"All right. The doctor said as long as you came to get it, you could have it," said the nurse. "But it's an obstinate case."

"My little grandson, he sit up there in the house all wrapped up, waiting by himself," Phoenix went on. "We is the only two left in the world. He suffer and it don't seem to put him back at all. He got a sweet look. He going to last. He wear a little patch quilt and peep out holding his mouth open like a little bird. I remembers so plain now. I not going to forget him again, no, the whole enduring time. I could tell him from all the others in creation."

"All right." The nurse was trying to hush her now. She brought her a bottle of medicine. "Charity," she said, making a check mark in a book.

Old Phoenix held the bottle close to her eyes, and then carefully put it into her pocket.

"I thank you," she said.

"It's Christmas time, Grandma," said the attendant. "Could I give you a few pennies out of my purse?"

"Five pennies is a nickel," said Phoenix stiffly.

"Here's a nickel," said the attendant.

Phoenix rose carefully and held out her hand. She received the nickel and then fished the other nickel out of her pocket and laid it beside the new one. She stared at her palm closely, with her head on one side.

Then she gave a tap with her cane on the floor.

"This is what come to me to do," she said. "I going to the store and buy my child a little windmill they sells, made out of paper. He going to find it hard to believe there such a thing in the world. I'll march myself back where he waiting, holding it straight up in this hand."

She lifted her free hand, gave a little nod, turned around, and walked out of the doctor's office. Then her slow step began on the stairs, going down.

STEP 9

WRITE YOUR PAPER

Just as with poetry, you might choose from any number of ways to write about short fiction. If you choose to write on a *single aspect* of a story, review your notes for the step that deals with the aspect you have selected. If you wanted to discuss the impact of setting in "Appointment in Samarra," for example, your notes for Step 4 would indicate that the action takes place in the Orient of long ago, with a market scene that could have come from the *Arabian Nights*. Perhaps your thesis might be that such an exotic setting was appropriate for a tale of fatality. One student, Bill Newman, chose to write about irony in "The Open Window." His analysis, found on page 79, gave him insights into other aspects of the story. (Other examples of themes dealing with a single aspect will be found in the sections on Drama—page 145—and on Poetry—page 45.)

If you decide to write on *several aspects* of a story, line up your notes from the appropriate steps, review them, and use them to develop your thesis. An example of this approach is provided by Eugenia Collins' discussion of two aspects of "A Worn Path" on pages 76–79. You will notice that she has used several steps to create her thesis.

You can begin to select your own topic by asking yourself a question about your response to the story. You might ask: What did I like best in the story? Whom did I feel was most believable? What made the story so effective? Write down your question and answer it, working with your answer until it is a full sentence expressing your response to the story: this can serve as part of the thesis for your paper.

Different types of papers can be written about a story or poem, even when they are based on the same steps. For example, Eugenia Collins used the steps dealing with setting and imagery in order to discuss love and compassion in "A Worn Path"; her paper is included at the end of this section. Another student wrote a paper of evaluation in which she used the same steps to substantiate her claim that setting is the most important aspect of that story. You may wish to work for a few minutes with this student's sample thesis in order to discover some techniques for working with your own:

> Setting in "A Worn Path" is effective; the descriptions are beautiful.

Underline the key words in the rough thesis. Jot down questions about each key word. Some of your questions will remind you to define key terms; others will raise points that you wish to expand. Group the questions and you will have the beginnings of an outline. Then you can go back to your worksheet notes, and to the story, in order to develop your points.

Look again at the sample thesis:

> <u>Setting</u> in "A Worn Path" is <u>effective</u>; the <u>descriptions</u> are <u>beautiful</u>.

Certainly, that sentence is too general; by making notes to yourself under each key word, however, you will find yourself refining your rough thesis as you clarify your ideas:

   I. Setting—the path on the Natchez Trace—the woods Phoenix walks through and the town she visits.

  II. Effective—so real, I am a part of Phoenix's world and I believe she really walked through the woods. Feel I know her after watching her struggle through the woods on her journey—what compassion and love she must have to make such a journey time and time again!

 III. Descriptions/Beautiful—imagery: primarily appeals to sight and sound, usually in descriptions of Phoenix and the country—more similes than metaphors; most images in comparisons.

      Partial list from story of sight images for comparison:

      Similes—walking—moving from side to side—like a pendulum in a grandfather clock (page 65)

      —tapping cane sounds meditative, like the chirping of a solitary little bird (page 65)

      —cane—limber as a buggy whip (page 65)

      —crossing log over creek like a festival figure in some parade (page 66)

      —crawling through barbed-wire fence like a baby trying to climb the steps (page 66)

      —quail walking around like pullets (page 67)

      —live oaks met, dark as a cave (page 68)

      —Phoenix fell in the ditch like a little puff of milkweed (page 68)

      —shadows hung from oak trees like curtains (page 70)

      —wrinkles in her skin shone like a bright net (page 71)

      —grandson peeping out of quilt holding his mouth open like a little bird (page 72)

      Metaphors—tree in pearly cloud of mistletoe (page 66)

> *Revised thesis:* The setting of "A Worn Path," as effectively presented in a series of visual comparisons, establishes the feeling that the reader is a part of Phoenix's world.

Now you are ready to make a rough outline and write the first draft of your paper. Remember to check your draft for coherence and to reexamine your thesis sentence before polishing and revising, as suggested in Step 10 of the Poetry section.

Similar techniques can be used to arrive at a thesis sentence for another type of theme. Use the "box" method illustrated in Step 10 of the Poetry section (and expanded in Step 9 of the Drama section) to sort your ideas and help create a thesis showing *comparison and contrast.* For example, you might want to discuss the ironic endings of "The Rabbits Who Caused All the Trouble" and "Appointment in Samarra." Your thesis sentence for a theme *exploring a problem* might deal with whether the moral at the end of Thurber's fable is to be taken literally or is another ironic aspect of the tale. Here, as in a theme of *evaluation,* the evidence you present must be based on your careful analysis of the work. For example, in claiming that the setting in "A Worn Path" is effective, Eugenia Collins found that she had to go back to her notes and to the story in order to substantiate her claim, as indicated in her revised thesis sentence.

LOVE AND COMPASSION IN EUDORA WELTY'S "A WORN PATH"

EUGENIA COLLINS

In her highly symbolic short story, "A Worn Path," [1] Eudora Welty tells the story of Phoenix, an ancient Negro woman, who is making a journey that she has made many times before, from her home in the country into the town of

---

[1] Eudora Welty, "A Worn Path," in *Selected Stories of Eudora Welty* (New York: Random House, 1943), p. 276.

Natchez, to get a soothing medicine for her little grandson, whose throat has been severely burned by lye. Her strenuous journey along the Natchez Trace—a rough trail through the back country of Mississippi, which had been worn by the wagons of the early settlers and, even earlier, by the feet of the Indians—would seem an impossible feat for such an old woman, but her great love and compassion for the child give her the strength and determination to go on in spite of all the obstacles in her path.

With carefully chosen, vividly descriptive phrases, Welty links the old woman with the Phoenix of Egyptian mythology, the great red and gold bird that lives for five hundred years and then destroys itself in a fire, only to be reborn from the ashes. "Her skin had a pattern all its own of numberless branching wrinkles . . . but a golden color ran underneath, and the two knobs of her cheeks were illumined by a yellow burning under the dark. Under the red rag her hair came down on her neck in the frailest of ringlets, still black, and with an odor like copper" (page 65).[2] She carries a cane that "made a grave and persistent noise in the still air, that seemed meditative like the chirping of a solitary little bird" (page 65).

Like her namesake, Phoenix also seems to be ageless. When she stops to refresh herself at a spring she says, "Nobody know who made this well, for it was here when I was born" (page 68). When the young hunter asks her how old she is, she answers, "There is no telling, mister, no telling" (page 69); but her extreme age is emphasized again when she tells the nurse in the doctor's office that she never went to school because "I was too old at the Surrender" (page 72).

All through this story of love and determination are overtones of myth and legend. Phoenix, fighting the many obstacles she must meet and overcome to get the needed medicine and return to her grandson, could be Jason in his quest for the Golden Fleece, or Ulysses struggling to return to his home after the Trojan War. As she goes along the path, she chants in an almost ceremonial way, "Out of my

[2] All page numbers refer to the reprinting of the story on pages 64–73 of the present volume.

way, all you foxes, owls, beetles, jack rabbits, coons and wild animals! . . . Keep out from under these feet, little bob-whites. . . . Keep the big wild hogs out of my path. . . . I got a long way" (page 65). When she comes to a log over a creek that she must cross, she is pictured again as a participant in a ceremonial journey: "Lifting her skirt, leveling her cane fiercely before her, like a festival figure in some parade, she began to march across" (page 66).

Strengthened by her love for her grandson, Phoenix not only is able to face and conquer the animals and other natural obstacles in her path, but in one scene she is symbolically depicted as able to defy even death itself. "Big dead trees, like black men with one arm, were standing in the purple stalks of the withered cotton field. There sat a buzzard.

" 'Who you watching?'

"In the furrow she made her way along" (pages 66–67).

Although Phoenix seems more at home in the natural world of the countryside, she is so intent upon her mission and fulfilled by the love and compassion that she feels for her little grandson that she is fully able to cope with the more artificial world of Natchez, with its red and green Christmas lights shining even in the daylight. She does not hesitate to ask a lady laden with packages to stop and tie her shoelaces, saying, "I doesn't mind asking a nice lady to tie up my shoe, when I gets out on the street" (page 70).

Welty emphasizes the love and compassion that Phoenix exhibits by contrasting her with the people she meets on her journey. The hunter cannot patronize her with his remark, "I know you old colored people! Wouldn't miss going to town to see Santa Claus!" (page 69). Phoenix knows that her mission is important; and he cannot belittle her, only himself. The women in the doctor's office who treat her with impatience and speak callously of the child as though his case were hopeless and her trip foolish, are met with a calm dignity and patience and seem only more uncaring by contrast.

When the attendant gives Phoenix a nickel, again the attempt to patronize her is unsuccessful, because she has an idea already in her mind of the wonderful use she will make of the money. " 'This is what come to me to do,' she said. 'I going to the store and buy my child a little wind- mill they sells, made out of paper. He going to find it hard to believe there such a thing in the world. I'll march myself back where he waiting, holding it straight up in this hand' " (page 73). And so she goes slowly out to begin her long journey home, this time like one of the ancient wise men, bearing a gift to the Child at Christmas.

Phoenix travels the worn path of human trouble and suffering that all humanity must travel; but she carries with her great compassion, strength, and courage. She has a deep love for humanity and faith in its future, affirmed by her description of her little grandson: "He suffer and it don't seem to put him back at all. He got a sweet look. He going to last" (page 72).

IRONY IN SAKI'S "THE OPEN WINDOW"

BILL NEWMAN

Perhaps the most memorable aspect of Saki's "The Open Window" [1] is its surprise—indeed, shock—ending. Much of the pleasure of the story comes from our awareness, not only of Vera's deception, but of the fact that we have been just as gullible as the unfortunate Framton. Only upon closer examination of the story do we realize that Saki has used concentric spheres of irony involving situation, characteriza- tion, style, and structure in order to prepare for the final irony of the twist ending.

Irony of situation centers upon Framton, the neurotic character with whom the reader is led to identify. The major irony here, of course, stems from the fact that Framton, who has gone to the country as part of his "nerve cure," receives a terrible fright while making his first neighborly visit, a

[1] Saki (H. H. Munro), "The Open Window," in *The Short Stories of Saki* (New York: Viking Press, 1930), pp. 288–91.

fright that undoubtedly will result in extensive damage to his nerves. Along with this basic irony of situation are several subordinate ironies that serve to reinforce the first. One of these is the fact that Framton, a misfit in the world of polite society, is forced by etiquette to go visiting, a duty it is obvious he would have preferred to avoid. It is also ironic that Framton's sister, wishing only the best for him, is responsible for the visit that ends in such horror.

Finally, it is ironic that Framton allows himself to be manipulated by both his sister and Vera, for in both cases he is aware, at least subconsciously, that he himself knows what is best for him. Of his sister's plans, "Privately he doubted . . . whether these formal visits on a succession of total strangers would do much towards helping the nerve cure which he was supposed to be undergoing" (page 56).[2] And just before Vera begins her calculated questions, Framton wonders whether the Sappletons, whose home he is visiting, come under "the nice division" of people his sister has known (page 56).

Closely related to the situational irony of the story is the irony used in the characterization, especially that of Framton. Contributing to this kind of irony is Saki's use of third-person limited point of view in most of the story, with only one brief glimpse into the mind of Vera, "when she judged that they had had sufficient silent communion" (page 56). Thus we are carefully led to identify with Framton throughout, and his shock at the end becomes our shock. This feeling of empathy with Framton is strengthened by the fact that Saki never entirely condemns his nervous protagonist. The author allows Framton a modicum of dignity by letting him protest occasionally—however feebly—his situation. For example, when Framton tells Vera that he has a letter of introduction from his sister, he does so "in a tone of distinct regret" (page 57). It is only after one has finished the tale that the inescapable truth strikes home: Framton is actually something of a fool; and the reader, having sympathized with him, feels equally foolish and humiliated.

[2] All page numbers refer to the reprinting of the story on pages 56–59 of the present volume.

While part of the irony of characterization in Saki's story comes from the point of view and the reader's consequent identification with Framton, an important part lies in the names given to the characters. The names are, in a sense, clues, but their full meaning is apparent only after one has finished reading the story. "Framton," for example, possibly alludes to the man's being framed by Vera, and "Nuttel" obviously implies that he is a nut. Mrs. Sappleton is made to seem a sap because she is taken in by the "short notice" romance Vera supplies at the end. " 'I expect it was the spaniel,' " Vera says straight-facedly, as we begin to grasp the full measure of her audacity. Her name, perhaps, is Saki's crowning ironic touch: "Truth" applied to this spinner of romances, this outright liar? Yet we see that she is not completely vicious because she only brings to light the foibles of others. Without their cooperation, her stories would not succeed. So in a sense "truth" is what Vera does discover: the genuine naiveté and gullibility concealed beneath the sophisticated social masks of her elders.

Like Saki's choice of names, the irony of his style in "The Open Window" contributes greatly to the artistry of the work. Most obvious in the pomposity applied most often to Framton, Saki's stylistic irony relies heavily on inflated diction, implication, and innuendo to influence the tone of the story independently of the plot. For instance, Framton "laboured under the tolerably wide-spread delusion that total strangers and chance acquaintances are hungry for the least detail of one's ailments and infirmities, their cause and cure." And Mrs. Sappleton replies to Framton's recital of his prescriptions "in a voice which only replaced a yawn at the last moment" (page 58).

This irony of style underlies the larger irony of structure that the reader recognizes fully only after finishing the story. Through his careful use of language, Saki creates a tightly woven fabric of suspense—and then reveals that it has been woven only to trick the reader. Before Framton's hasty exit, Saki gives no substantial hint that the hunters are still alive. So the final irony represents the culmination of all the ironies, completes the structure of the story, and involves us in a way that, we recognize wryly, puts us on a level with the wretched Framton. We imagine Saki somewhere laughing. But he invites us to laugh with him.

SUGGESTIONS FOR WRITING

I. Papers on a single aspect:
1. Point of view in "A Worn Path" (see Step 3)
2. Point of view in "The Open Window" (Step 3)
3. Setting in "Appointment in Samarra" (Step 4)
4. Setting in "The Open Window" (Step 4)
5. Characterization in "The Rabbits Who Caused All the Trouble" (Step 5)
6. Characterization in "The Open Window" (Step 5)
7. Plot and structure in any of the stories (Step 6)
8. Imagery and rhetorical devices in "The Open Window" (Step 7)
9. Imagery and rhetorical devices in "A Worn Path" (Step 7)
10. Symbol in "Appointment in Samarra" (Step 8)
11. Symbol in "The Rabbits Who Caused All the Trouble" (Step 8)

II. Papers on more than one aspect:
1. Point of view and characterization in:
   a. "The Open Window"
   b. "A Worn Path"
2. Imagery and symbolism in "A Worn Path"
3. Plot and setting in "Appointment in Samarra"

III. Papers of comparison and contrast:
1. Irony in "Appointment in Samarra" and "The Open Window"
2. Point of view and characterization in "The Open Window" and "A Worn Path"

IV. Papers exploring a problem:
1. What is the function of the moral of Thurber's fable, "The Rabbits Who Caused All the Trouble?"
2. Is the motif of a journey symbolic in "A Worn Path"?

V. Papers of explication: From any story you are studying, particularly a long story, choose a passage and explicate it as you did a poem. Particularly effective for this type of theme would be a passage that includes imagery or rhetorical devices within the description or dialogue. For example, some critics have noted the almost poetic quality of Phoenix's speeches to herself in "A Worn Path." Or choose a very short story and apply to it each of the steps for analysis discussed in this section; you can also apply each step to a long story, but you will probably have to select passages from it as examples for the various steps.

VI. Papers of evaluation: Evaluate any story you are studying. You might wish to review the sample notes on "A Worn Path" in Step 9, decide for yourself whether setting is effective in the story, and write an evaluation using your own thesis sentence.

Section III
Analyzing and Writing About a PLAY

Unlike a poem or a short story, which exist only on the printed page, plays have a double life: they can be seen and heard as well as read. So although you will read the play you want to write about as you would any other piece of literature, you should remember that the play was written for the theater and the dialogue of the actors always accompanies action that the theater audience can see.

While there is no substitute for the vivid experience of seeing and hearing what is happening onstage, reading the play has certain advantages too. In the theater you cannot yell, "Stop! Repeat that murder!"—or kiss, or conversation planning a jewel theft. After the play, we often think we would like to see a couple of scenes again just to see how the playwright plotted the action so that the ending was inevitable. In reading a play carefully, you can repeat the murder or the kiss or the jewel theft as many times as you want. You can see precisely how the playwright mixed the ingredients of character, setting, and plot to draw a particular reaction from the audience. So, although in reading a play you miss the excitement of the interaction between actors and audience, you can understand what the playwright did to make that excitement possible.

STEP 1

READ THE PLAY CAREFULLY

Modern theater audiences read a program before the play begins in order to learn the *setting* (when and where the action takes place) and the *dramatis personae* (names of the characters). Before printed programs were available, a theater audience picked up most of this information during the opening moments of the play. Since you cannot see the visual clues the playwright imagined for the theater audience, you must get as much information as you can from the text of the play you are analyzing.

The Proposal, a one-act play by the great nineteenth-century Russian playwright Anton Chekhov, is reprinted below. As you read it, follow the suggestions given in this step. Then you can analyze the play by following the remaining steps in this chapter.

First, note the title and when and where the play was written. *The Proposal,* for example, was written in the 1880s in Russia. Knowing this, we will expect the play to be about a marriage proposal but we will not expect names like John and Mary or a proposal made during a drive-in movie.

Read through the list of characters. If you notice any obvious relationships that might be important, mark them in some way. For instance, in a play by Shakespeare, where male characters are listed before female, you can bracket husband-and-wife or brother-and-sister couples. Sometimes important facts follow the names of the characters, as in this list for *The Proposal:*

STEPHEN CHUBUKOV, a landowner
NATASHA, his daughter, aged 25
IVAN LOMOV, a landowning neighbour of Chubukov's, hefty and
   well-nourished, but a hypochondriac

*The action takes place in the drawing-room of Chubukov's country-
   house*

In *The Proposal* Chekhov has included a brief note after each name in the list of characters. In many plays, however, this kind of description is omitted. In that case, as you read through the play—especially if it is very long—it is often helpful to turn back to the list of characters and add your own explanatory notes. If the book is not your own, make a list of important characters on a worksheet and write your notes on that.

Note the *setting* (when and where the action takes place) if it is given. Modern playwrights often give important information in their descriptions of the stage settings as well as of the characters. Note the parts of these descriptions that seem most important. In *The Proposal,* the action takes place in the drawing-room of Chubukov's country-house, which tells us that the Chubukovs must be rich: not only is the country-house large enough to have a drawing-room, but "country-house" implies that Chubukov also owns a town-house.

As you read the play, note act and scene changes; they tell you where the action is taking place. Of course, not all plays are divided into acts. *The Proposal,* for instance, has only one act, though it is divided into scenes. You should also note lines of dialogue and indications of action that seem important even on a first reading. As you study the play further by following the rest of the steps in this section, you will discover why the items you have marked are important.

In reading *The Proposal,* you might make notes like these:

SCENE II

[LOMOV, *alone.*]

Lomov sits alone, trying to talk himself into marrying N. She's not his ideal woman but he thinks marriage will cure his nervous symptoms.

LOMOV. I feel cold, I'm shaking like a leaf. Make up your mind, that's the great thing. If you keep chewing things over, dithering on the brink, arguing the toss and waiting for your ideal woman or true love to come along, you'll never get hitched up. Brrr! I'm cold. Natasha's a good housewife. She's not bad-looking and she's an educated girl—what more can you ask? But I'm so jumpy, my ears have started buzzing. [*Drinks water.*] And get married

L's not exactly head-over-heels in love. He's thinking of himself not of N.

I must. In the first place, I'm thirty-five years old—a critical age, so to speak. Secondly, I should lead a proper, regular life. I've heart trouble and constant palpitations, I'm irritable and nervous as a kitten. See how my lips are trembling now? See my right eyelid twitch? But my nights are the worst thing. No sooner do I get in bed and start dozing off than I have a sort of shooting pain in my left side. It goes right through my shoulder and head. Out I leap like a lunatic, walk about a bit, then lie down again —but the moment I start dropping off I get this pain in my side again. And it happens twenty times over.

It is often helpful—especially if the play you are reading is long—to write a running synopsis of what is happening onstage in the margins of your text or on your worksheet. Star whatever you think is especially interesting or significant. Since many of the considerations that apply to poetry and fiction also apply to drama, the study you have made of poems and stories will alert you to important passages and words in your play. A running synopsis of the first three scenes of *The Proposal* might read like this:

Scene 1 Lomov visits Chubukov to ask for his daughter's hand in marriage. Chubukov agrees, assuring Lomov that Natasha will jump at the chance.

Scene 2 Lomov sits alone, trying to talk himself into marrying Natasha. Even though she's not his ideal woman, he thinks marriage will cure his nervous symptoms.

Scene 3 Natasha comes in. Lomov tries to propose, but they get into a long, nasty argument, each claiming legal ownership of Oxpen Field.

THE PROPOSAL

A Farce in One Act (*1888–1889*)

ANTON CHEKHOV (1860–1904)

Characters

STEPHEN CHUBUKOV, a landowner
NATASHA, his daughter, aged 25
IVAN LOMOV, a landowning neighbour of Chubukov's,
  hefty and well-nourished, but a hypochondriac

The action takes place in the drawing-room of Chubukov's country-house

SCENE I

[CHUBUKOV *and* LOMOV; *the latter comes in wearing evening dress and white gloves.*]

CHUBUKOV [*going to meet him*]. Why, it's Ivan Lomov—or do my eyes deceive me, old boy? Delighted. [*Shakes hands.*] I say, old bean, this is a surprise! How *are* you?

LOMOV. All right, thanks. And how might you be?

CHUBUKOV. Not so bad, dear boy. Good of you to ask and so on. Now, you simply must sit down. Never neglect the neighbours, old bean—what? But why so formal, old boy—the tails, the gloves and so on? Not going anywhere, are you, dear man?

LOMOV. Only coming here, my dear Chubukov.

CHUBUKOV. Then why the tails, my dear fellow? Why make such a great thing of it?

LOMOV. Well, look, the point is—. [*Takes his arm.*] I came to ask a favour, my dear Chubukov, if it's not too much bother. I have had the privilege of enlisting your help more than once, and you've always, as it were—but I'm so nervous, sorry. I'll drink some water, my dear Chubukov. [*Drinks water.*]

CHUBUKOV [*aside*]. He's come to borrow money. Well, there's nothing doing! [*To him.*] What's the matter, my dear fellow?

LOMOV. Well, you see, my chear Dubukov—my dear Chubukov, I mean, sorry—that's to say, I'm terribly jumpy, as you see. In fact only you can help me, though I don't deserve it, of course, and, er, have no claims on you either.

CHUBUKOV. Now don't muck about with it, old bean. Let's have it. Well?

LOMOV. Certainly, this instant. The fact is, I'm here to ask for the hand of your daughter Natasha.

CHUBUKOV [*delightedly*]. My dear Lomov! Say that again, old horse, I didn't quite catch it.

LOMOV. I have the honour to ask——

CHUBUKOV [*interrupting him*]. My dear old boy! I'm delighted and so on, er, and so forth—what? [*Embraces and kisses him.*] I've long wanted it, it's always been my wish. [*Sheds a tear.*] I've always loved you as a son, dear boy. May you both live happily ever after and so on. As for me, I've always wanted—. But why do I stand around like a blithering idiot? I'm tickled pink, I really am! Oh, I most cordially—. I'll go and call Natasha and so forth.

LOMOV [*very touched*]. My dear Chubukov, what do you think— can I count on a favourable response?

CHUBUKOV. What—her turn down a good-looking young fellow like you! Not likely! I bet she's crazy about you and so on. One moment. [*Goes out.*]

SCENE II

[LOMOV, *alone.*]

LOMOV. I feel cold, I'm shaking like a leaf. Make up your mind, that's the great thing. If you keep chewing things over, dithering on the brink, arguing the toss and waiting for your ideal woman or true love to come along, you'll never get hitched up. Brrr! I'm cold. Natasha's a good housewife. She's not bad-looking and she's an educated girl—what more can you ask? But I'm so jumpy, my ears have started buzzing. [*Drinks water.*] And get married I must. In the first place, I'm thirty-five years old—a critical age, so to speak. Secondly, I should lead a proper, regular life. I've heart trouble and constant palpitations, I'm irritable and nervous as a kitten. See how my lips are trembling now? See my right eyelid twitch? But my nights are the worst thing. No sooner do I get in bed and start dozing off than I have a sort of shooting pain in my left side. It goes right through my shoulder and head. Out I leap like a lunatic, walk about a bit, then lie down again—but the moment I start dropping off I get this pain in my side again. And it happens twenty times over.

SCENE III

[NATASHA *and* LOMOV.]

NATASHA [*comes in*]. Oh, it's you. That's funny, Father said it was a dealer collecting some goods or something. Good morning, Mr. Lomov.

LOMOV. And good morning to you, my dear Miss Chubukov.

NATASHA. Excuse my apron, I'm not dressed for visitors. We've been shelling peas—we're going to dry them. Why haven't you been over for so long? Do sit down. [*They sit.*] Will you have lunch?

LOMOV. Thanks, I've already had some.

NATASHA. Or a smoke? Here are some matches. It's lovely weather, but it rained so hard yesterday—the men were idle all day. How much hay have you cut? I've been rather greedy, you know—I mowed all mine, and now I'm none too happy in case it rots. I should have hung on. But what's this I see? Evening dress, it seems. That *is* a surprise! Going dancing or something?

You're looking well, by the way—but why on earth go round in that get-up?

LOMOV [*agitated*]. Well, you see, my dear Miss Chubukov. The fact is, I've decided to ask you to—er, lend me your ears. You're bound to be surprised—angry, even. But I—. [*Aside.*] I feel terribly cold.

NATASHA. What's up then? [*Pause.*] Well?

LOMOV. I'll try to cut it short. Miss Chubukov, you are aware that I have long been privileged to know your family—since I was a boy, in fact. My dear departed aunt and her husband— from whom, as you are cognizant, I inherited the estate— always entertained the deepest respect for your father and dear departed mother. We Lomovs and Chubukovs have always been on the friendliest terms—you might say we've been pretty thick. And what's more, as you are also aware, we own closely adjoining properties. You may recall that my land at Oxpen Field is right next to your birch copse.

NATASHA. Sorry to butt in, but you refer to Oxpen Field as "yours"? Surely you're not serious!

LOMOV. I am, madam.

NATASHA. Well, I like that! Oxpen Field is ours, it isn't yours.

LOMOV. You're wrong, my dear Miss Chubukov, that's my land.

NATASHA. This is news to me. How can it be yours?

LOMOV. How? What do you mean? I'm talking about Oxpen Field, that wedge of land between your birch copse and Burnt Swamp.

NATASHA. That's right. It's our land.

LOMOV. No, you're mistaken, my dear Miss Chubukov. It's mine.

NATASHA. Oh, come off it, Mr. Lomov. How long has it been yours?

LOMOV. How long? As long as I can remember—it's always been ours.

NATASHA. I say, this really is a bit steep!

LOMOV. But you have only to look at the deeds, my dear Miss Chubukov. Oxpen Field once *was* in dispute, I grant you, but it's mine now—that's common knowledge, and no argument about it. If I may explain, my aunt's grandmother made over that field rent free to your father's grandfather's labourers for their indefinite use in return for firing her bricks. Now, your great-grandfather's people used the place rent free for forty years or so, and came to look on it as their own. Then when the government land settlement was brought out——

NATASHA. No, that's all wrong. My grandfather and great-grandfather both claimed the land up to Burnt Swamp as theirs. So Oxpen Field was ours. Why argue? That's what I can't see. This is really rather aggravating.

LOMOV. I'll show you the deeds, Miss Chubukov.

NATASHA. Oh, you must be joking or having me on. This *is* a nice surprise! You own land for nearly three hundred years, then someone ups and tells you it's not yours! Mr. Lomov, I'm sorry, but I simply can't believe my ears. I don't mind about the field—it's only the odd twelve acres, worth the odd three hundred roubles. But it's so unfair—that's what infuriates me. I can't stand unfairness, I don't care what you say.

LOMOV. Do hear me out, please! With due respect, your great-grandfather's people baked bricks for my aunt's grandmother, as I've already told you. Now, my aunt's grandmother wanted to do them a favour——

NATASHA. Grandfather, grandmother, aunt—it makes no sense to me. The field's ours, and that's that.

LOMOV. It's mine.

NATASHA. It's ours! Argue till the cows come home, put on tailcoats by the dozen for all I care—it'll still be ours, ours, ours! I'm not after your property, but I don't propose losing mine either, and I don't care what you think!

LOMOV. My dear Miss Chubukov, it's not that I need that field—it's the principle of the thing. If you want it, have it. Take it as a gift.

NATASHA. But it's mine to give *you* if I want—it's my property. This is odd, to put it mildly. We always thought you such a good neighbour and friend, Mr. Lomov. We lent you our threshing-machine last year, and couldn't get our own threshing done till November in consequence. We might be gipsies, the way you treat us. Making me a present of my own property! I'm sorry, but that's not exactly neighbourly of you. In fact, if you ask me, it's sheer howling cheek.

LOMOV. So I'm trying to pinch your land now, am I? It's not my habit, madam, to grab land that isn't mine, and I won't have anyone say it is! [*Quickly goes to the carafe and drinks some water.*] Oxpen Field belongs to me.

NATASHA. That's a lie, it's ours.

LOMOV. It's mine.

NATASHA. That's a lie and I'll nail it! I'll send my men to cut that field this very day.

LOMOV. What do you say?

NATASHA. My men will be out on that field today!

LOMOV. Too right, they'll be out! Out on their ear!

NATASHA. You'd never dare.

LOMOV [*clutches his heart*]. Oxpen Field belongs to me, do you hear? It's mine!

NATASHA. Kindly stop shouting. By all means yell yourself blue in the face when you're in your own home, but I'll thank you to keep a civil tongue in your head in this house.

LOMOV. Madam, if I hadn't got these awful, agonizing palpitations and this throbbing in my temples, I'd give you a piece of my mind! [*Shouts.*] Oxpen Field belongs to me.

NATASHA. To us, you mean!

LOMOV. It's mine.

NATASHA. It's ours!

LOMOV. Mine!

SCENE IV

[*The above and* CHUBUKOV.]

CHUBUKOV [*coming in*]. What's going on, what's all the row in aid of?

NATASHA. Father, who owns Oxpen Field? Would you mind telling this gentleman? Is it his or ours?

CHUBUKOV [*to* LOMOV]. That field's ours, old cock!

LOMOV. Now look here, Chubukov, how can it be? You at least might show some sense! My aunt's grandmother made over that field to your grandfather's farm-labourers rent free on a temporary basis. Those villagers had the use of the land for forty years and came to think of it as theirs, but when the settlement came out——

CHUBUKOV. Now hang on, dear man, you forget one thing. That field was in dispute and so forth even in those days—and that's why the villagers paid your grandmother no rent and so on. But now it belongs to us, every dog in the district knows that, what? You can't have seen the plans.

LOMOV. It's mine and I'll prove it.

CHUBUKOV. Oh no you won't, my dear good boy.

LOMOV. Oh yes, I will.

CHUBUKOV. No need to shout, old bean. Shouting won't prove anything, what? I'm not after your property, but I don't propose losing mine, either. Why on earth should I? If it comes to that, old sausage, if you're set on disputing the field and so on, I'd rather give it to the villagers than you. So there.

LOMOV. This makes no sense to me. What right have you to give other people's property away?

CHUBUKOV. Permit me to be the best judge of that. Now, look here, young feller-me-lad—I'm not used to being spoken to like this, what? I'm twice your age, boy, and I'll thank you to talk to me without getting hot under the collar and so forth.

LOMOV. Oh, really, you must take me for a fool. You're pulling my leg. You say my land's yours, then you expect me to keep my temper and talk things over amicably. I call this downright unneighbourly, Chubukov. You're not a neighbour, you're a thoroughgoing shark!

CHUBUKOV. I *beg* your pardon! What did you say?

NATASHA. Father, send the men out to mow that field this very instant!

CHUBUKOV [*to* LOMOV]. What was it you said, sir?

NATASHA. Oxpen Field's ours and I won't let it go, I won't, I won't!

LOMOV. We'll see about that! I'll have the law on you!

CHUBUKOV. You will, will you? Then go right ahead, sir, and so forth, go ahead and sue, sir! Oh, I know your sort! Just what you're angling for and so on, isn't it—a court case, what? Quite the legal eagle, aren't you? Your whole family's always been litigation-mad, every last one of 'em!

LOMOV. I'll thank you not to insult my family. We Lomovs have always been honest, we've none of us been had up for embezzlement like your precious uncle.

CHUBUKOV. The Lomovs have always been mad as hatters!

NATASHA. Yes! All of you! Mad!

CHUBUKOV. Your grandfather drank like a fish, and your younger Aunt What's-her-name—Nastasya—ran off with an architect and so on.

LOMOV. And your mother was a cripple. [*Clutches his heart.*] There's that shooting pain in my side, and a sort of blow on the head. Heavens alive! Water!

CHUBUKOV. Your father gambled and ate like a pig!

NATASHA. Your aunt was a most frightful busybody!

LOMOV. My left leg's gone to sleep. And you're a very slippery customer. Oh my heart! And it's common knowledge that at election time you bri—. I'm seeing stars. Where's my hat?

NATASHA. What a rotten, beastly, filthy thing to say.

CHUBUKOV. You're a thoroughly nasty, cantankerous, hypocritical piece of work, what? Yes, sir!

LOMOV. Ah, there's my hat. My heart—. Which way do I go? Where's the door? Oh, I think I'm dying. I can hardly drag one foot after another. [*Moves to the door.*]

CHUBUKOV [*after him*]. You need never set either of those feet in my house again, sir.

NATASHA. Go ahead and sue, we'll see what happens.

[LOMOV *goes out staggering.*]

SCENE V

[CHUBUKOV *and* NATASHA.]

CHUBUKOV. Oh, blast it! [*Walks up and down in agitation.*]

NATASHA. The rotten cad! So much for trusting the dear neighbours!

CHUBUKOV. Scruffy swine!

NATASHA. He's an out-and-out monster! Pinches your land and then has the cheek to swear at you!

CHUBUKOV. And this monstrosity, this blundering oaf, has the immortal rind to come here with his proposal and so on, what? A proposal! I ask you!

NATASHA. A proposal, did you say?

CHUBUKOV. Not half I did! He came here to propose to you!

NATASHA. Propose? To me? Then why didn't you say so before?

CHUBUKOV. That's why he dolled himself up in tails. Damn popinjay! Twerp!

NATASHA. Me? Propose to me? Oh! [*Falls in an armchair and groans.*] Bring him back! Bring him back! Bring him back, I tell you!

CHUBUKOV. Bring who back?

NATASHA. Hurry up, be quick, I feel faint. Bring him back. [*Has hysterics.*]

CHUBUKOV. What's this? What do you want? [*Clutches his head.*] Oh, misery! I might as well go and boil my head! I'm fed up with them!

NATASHA. I'm dying. Bring him back!

CHUBUKOV. Phew! All right then. No need to howl. [*Runs out.*]

NATASHA [*alone, groans*]. What have we done! Bring him, bring him back!

CHUBUKOV [*runs in*]. He'll be here in a moment and so on, damn him! Phew! You talk to him—I don't feel like it, what?

NATASHA [*groans*]. Bring him back!

CHUBUKOV [*shouts*]. He's coming, I tell you.
> My fate, ye gods, is just too bad—
> To be a grown-up daughter's dad!

I'll cut my throat, I'll make a point of it. We've sworn at the man, insulted him and kicked him out of the house. And it was all your doing.

NATASHA. It was *not,* it was yours!

CHUBUKOV. So now it's my fault, what?

[LOMOV *appears in the doorway.*]

CHUBUKOV. All right, now you talk to him. [*Goes out.*]

SCENE VI

[NATASHA *and* LOMOV.]

LOMOV [*comes in, exhausted*]. My heart's fairly thumping away, my leg's gone to sleep and there's this pain in my side——

NATASHA. I'm sorry we got a bit excited, Mr. Lomov. I've just remembered—Oxpen Field really does belong to you.

LOMOV. My heart's fairly thumping away. That field's mine. I've a nervous tic in both eyes.

NATASHA. The field *is* yours, certainly. Do sit down. [*They sit.*] We were mistaken.

LOMOV. This is a question of principle. It's not the land I mind about, it's the principle of the thing.

NATASHA. Just so, the principle. Now let's change the subject.

LOMOV. Especially as I can prove it. My aunt's grandmother gave your father's grandfather's villagers——

NATASHA. All right, that'll do. [*Aside.*] I don't know how to start. [*To him.*] Thinking of going shooting soon?

LOMOV. Yes, I'm thinking of starting on the woodcock after the harvest, my dear Miss Chubukov. I say, have you heard? What awful bad luck! You know my dog Tracker? He's gone lame.

NATASHA. Oh, I am sorry. How did it happen?

LOMOV. I don't know. Either it must be a sprain, or the other dogs bit him. [*Sighs.*] My best dog, to say nothing of what he set me back! Do you know, I gave Mironov a hundred and twenty-five roubles for him?

NATASHA. Then you were had, Mr. Lomov.

LOMOV. He came very cheap if you ask me—he's a splendid dog.

NATASHA. Father only gave eighty-five roubles for Rover. And Rover's a jolly sight better dog than Tracker, you'll agree.

LOMOV. Rover better than Tracker! Oh, come off it! [*Laughs.*] Rover a better dog than Tracker!

NATASHA. Of course he is. Rover's young, it's true, and not yet in his prime. But you could search the best kennels in the county without finding a nippier animal, or one with better points.

LOMOV. I am sorry, Miss Chubukov, but you forget he has a short lower jaw, and a dog like that can't grip.

NATASHA. Oh, can't he! That's news to me!

LOMOV. He has a weak chin, you can take that from me.

NATASHA. Why, have you measured it?

LOMOV. Yes, I have. Naturally he'll do for coursing, but when it comes to retrieving, that's another story.

NATASHA. In the first place, Rover has a good honest coat on him, and a pedigree as long as your arm. As for that mud-coloured, piebald animal of yours, his antecedents are anyone's guess, quite apart from him being ugly as a broken-down old cart-horse.

LOMOV. Old he may be, but I wouldn't swap him for half a dozen Rovers—not on your life! Tracker's a real dog, and Rover—why, it's absurd to argue. The kennels are lousy with Rovers, he'd be dear at twenty-five roubles.

NATASHA. You *are* in an awkward mood today, Mr. Lomov. First you decide our field is yours, now you say Tracker's better than Rover. I dislike people who won't speak their mind. Now, you know perfectly well that Rover's umpteen times better than that—yes, that stupid Tracker. So why say the opposite?

LOMOV. I see you don't credit me with eyes or brains, Miss Chubukov. Well, get it in your head that Rover has a weak chin.

NATASHA. That's not true.

LOMOV. Oh yes it is!

NATASHA [*shouts*]. Oh no it isn't.

LOMOV. Don't you raise your voice at me, madam.

NATASHA. Then don't you talk such utter balderdash! Oh, this is infuriating! It's time that measly Tracker was put out of his misery—and you compare him with Rover!

LOMOV. I can't go on arguing, sorry—it's my heart.

NATASHA. Men who argue most about sport, I've noticed, are always the worst sportsmen.

LOMOV. Will you kindly hold your trap, madam—my heart's breaking in two. [*Shouts.*] You shut up!

NATASHA. I'll do nothing of the sort till you admit Rover's a hundred times better than Tracker.

LOMOV. A hundred times worse, more like! I hope Rover drops dead! Oh, my head, my eye, my shoulder——

NATASHA. That half-wit Tracker doesn't need to drop dead—he's pretty well a walking corpse already.

LOMOV [*weeps*]. Shut up! I'm having a heart attack!

NATASHA. I will *not* shut up!

SCENE VII

[*The above and* CHUBUKOV.]

CHUBUKOV [*comes in*]. What is it this time?

NATASHA. Father, I want an honest answer: which is the better dog, Rover or Tracker?

LOMOV. Will you kindly tell us just one thing, Chubukov: has Rover got a weak chin or hasn't he? Yes or no?

CHUBUKOV. What if he has? As if that mattered! Seeing he's only the best dog in the county and so on.

LOMOV. Tracker's better, and you know it! Be honest!

CHUBUKOV. Keep your shirt on, dear man. Now look here. Tracker has got some good qualities, what? He's a pedigree dog, has firm paws, steep haunches and so forth. But that dog has two serious faults if you want to know, old bean: he's old and he's pug-nosed.

LOMOV. I'm sorry—it's my heart! Let's just look at the facts. You may recall that Tracker was neck and neck with the Count's Swinger on Maruskino Green when Rover was a good half-mile behind.

CHUBUKOV. He dropped back because the Count's huntsman fetched him a crack with his whip.

LOMOV. Serve him right. Hounds are all chasing the fox and Rover has to start worrying a sheep!

CHUBUKOV. That's not true, sir. I've got a bad temper, old boy, and the fact is—let's please stop arguing, what? He hit him because everyone hates the sight of another man's dog. Oh yes they do. Loathe 'em, they do. And you're no one to talk either, sir! The moment you spot a better dog than the wretched Tracker, you always try to start something and, er, so forth—what? I don't forget, you see.

LOMOV. Nor do I, sir.

CHUBUKOV [*mimics him*]. "Nor do I, sir." What is it you don't forget then?

LOMOV. My heart! My leg's gone to sleep. I can't go on.

NATASHA [*mimics him*]. "My heart!" Call yourself a sportsman! You should be lying on the kitchen stove squashing black-beetles, not fox-hunting. His heart!

CHUBUKOV. Some sportsman, I must say! With that heart you should stay at home, not bob around in the saddle, what? I wouldn't mind if you hunted properly, but you only turn out to pick quarrels and annoy the hounds and so on. I have a bad temper, so let's change the subject. You're no sportsman, sir—what?

LOMOV. What about you then? You only turn out so you can get in the Count's good books and intrigue against people. Oh, my heart! You're a slippery customer, sir!

CHUBUKOV. What's that, sir? Oh, I am, am I? [*Shouts.*] Hold your tongue!

LOMOV. You artful old dodger!

CHUBUKOV. Why, you young puppy!

LOMOV. Nasty old fogy! Canting hypocrite!

CHUBUKOV. Shut up, or I'll pot you like a ruddy partridge. And I'll use a dirty gun too, you idle gasbag!

LOMOV. And it's common knowledge that—oh, my heart—your wife used to beat you. Oh, my leg! My head! I can see stars! I can't stand up!

CHUBUKOV. And your housekeeper has you eating out of her hand!

LOMOV. Oh, oh! My heart's bursting. My shoulder seems to have come off—where is the thing? I'm dying. [*Falls into an armchair.*] Fetch a doctor. [*Faints.*]

CHUBUKOV. Why, you young booby! Hot air merchant! I think I'm going to faint. [*Drinks water.*] I feel unwell.

NATASHA. Calls himself a sportsman and can't even sit on a horse! [*To her father.*] Father, what's the matter with him? Father, have a look. [*Screeches.*] Mr. Lomov! He's dead!

CHUBUKOV. I feel faint. I can't breathe! Give me air!

NATASHA. He's dead. [*Tugs* LOMOV's *sleeve.*] Mr. Lomov, Mr. Lomov! What have we done? He's dead. [*Falls into an armchair.*] Fetch a doctor, a doctor! [*Has hysterics.*]

CHUBUKOV. Oh! What's happened? What's the matter?

NATASHA [*groans*]. He's dead! Dead!

CHUBUKOV. Who's dead? [*Glancing at* LOMOV.] My God, you're right! Water! A doctor! [*Holds a glass to* LOMOV's *mouth.*] Drink! No, he's not drinking. He must be dead, and so forth. Oh, misery, misery! Why don't I put a bullet in my brain? Why did I never get round to cutting my throat? What am I waiting for? Give me a knife! A pistol! [LOMOV *makes a move-*

ment.] I think he's coming 'round. Drink some water! That's right.

LOMOV. I can see stars! There's a sort of mist. Where am I?

CHUBUKOV. Hurry up and get married and—oh, to hell with you! She says yes. [*Joins their hands.*] She says yes, and so forth. You have my blessing, and so on. Just leave me in peace, that's all.

LOMOV. Eh? What? [*Raising himself.*] Who?

CHUBUKOV. She says yes. Well, what about it? Kiss each other and—oh, go to hell!

NATASHA [*groans*]. He's alive. Yes, yes, yes! I agree.

CHUBUKOV. Come on, kiss.

LOMOV. Eh? Who? [*Kisses* NATASHA.] Very nice too. I say, what's all this about? Oh, I see—. My heart! I'm seeing stars! Miss Chubukov, I'm so happy. [*Kisses her hand.*] My leg's gone to sleep.

NATASHA. I, er, I'm happy too.

CHUBUKOV. Oh, what a weight off my mind! Phew!

NATASHA. Still, you must admit now that Tracker's not a patch on Rover.

LOMOV. Oh yes he is!

NATASHA. Oh no he isn't!

CHUBUKOV. You can see those two are going to live happily ever after! Champagne!

LOMOV. He's better.

NATASHA. He's worse, worse, worse.

CHUBUKOV [*trying to shout them down*]. Champagne, champagne, champagne!

Curtain

STEP 2

CLASSIFY THE PLAY

Plays may be roughly grouped into *comedies* and *tragedies*. Comedies end happily, traditionally with a wedding, and aim to cause laughter at funny situations. Tragedies end unhappily, nearly always with the death or defeat of the main character, called the *tragic hero* (see Step 5). According to Aristotle's discussion of drama in the *Poetics*, the purpose of a tragedy is to arouse pity and fear in the audience and to cause the *catharsis*, or purging, of these emotions. Although no one is precisely certain what Aristotle meant by this, nearly everyone has experienced the emotional draining that results from having gotten so intensely involved with the actions of a play that we seem to have lived them ourselves.

Not all plays fit neatly into these two broad categories. A *tragicomedy* is a play in which the plot is serious enough to be suitable for a tragedy, but which has the happy ending of a comedy. Deliberately less believable (see Section II, Step 5) than comedy is *farce*, in which caricaturelike characters involved in outrageously improbable actions provoke only laughter. For example, in *The Proposal*, which Chekhov called a farce, he has pushed to the extreme limits of probability the cliché that all women are after a husband by making Lomov so unappealing.

As farce is to comedy, *melodrama* is to tragedy. It may deal with the same situation as tragedy, but always manages to arrange the survival or triumph of the *protagonist* (the main character) in the end—even if the way in which this is done is highly improbable. Television soap operas, in which the main characters must survive for the next episodes, are nearly always melodramas. Actors in both farce and melodrama often overact in order to make the situations in which they are involved as exaggerated as possible.

A short play may include many tragic elements, though it does not have enough scope for the examination of character that is necessary for a true tragedy. Such a play is John Millington Synge's *Riders to the Sea,* which is reprinted below.

Modern playwrights often write plays that do not precisely fit the standard labels. Writers of the theater of the absurd—Eugene Ionesco, Samuel Beckett, and Edward Albee, for example—try to depict the essential absurdity of the human condition by abandoning realistic form and the rational devices of the traditional plot, such as a cause-and-effect progression. Writers of the theater of cruelty, originated by Antonin Artaud in the 1930s, rely less on dialogue than on spectacle and sound to shock the spectators and make them feel that they are actively participating in the drama. Despite such playwrights' rejection of traditional forms, however, many of their productions can be usefully studied by means of traditional techniques, even though the resulting analysis may consist largely of negative statements.

Use the techniques given in Step 1 as you read *Riders to the Sea.* At this point in your study of any play you can note its type on your worksheet. The rest of the steps in this section will help you to analyze it more fully.

RIDERS TO THE SEA

JOHN MILLINGTON SYNGE (1871–1909)

Persons in the Play

MAURYA (*an old woman*)
BARTLEY (*her son*)
CATHLEEN (*her daughter*)
NORA (*a younger daughter*)
MEN and WOMEN

SCENE. *An Island off the West of Ireland.*
(*Cottage kitchen, with nets, oil-skins, spinning wheel, some new boards standing by the wall, etc. Cathleen, a girl of*

about twenty, finishes kneading cake, and puts it down in
the pot-oven by the fire; then wipes her hands, and begins
to spin at the wheel. Nora, a young girl, puts her head in
at the door.)

NORA (*in a low voice*). Where is she?

CATHLEEN. She's lying down, God help her, and may be sleeping,
if she's able.

[*Nora comes in softly, and takes a bundle from under her*
shawl.]

CATHLEEN (*spinning the wheel rapidly*). What is it you have?

NORA. The young priest is after bringing them. It's a shirt and a
plain stocking were got off a drowned man in Donegal.

[*Cathleen stops her wheel with a sudden movement, and*
leans out to listen.]

NORA. We're to find out if it's Michael's they are, some time
herself will be down looking by the sea.

CATHLEEN. How would they be Michael's, Nora? How would he
go the length of that way to the far north?

NORA. The young priest says he's known the like of it. "If it's
Michael's they are," says he, "you can tell herself he's got a
clean burial by the grace of God, and if they're not his, let no
one say a word about them, for she'll be getting her death,"
says he, "with crying and lamenting."

[*The door which Nora half closed is blown open by a gust*
of wind.]

CATHLEEN (*looking out anxiously*). Did you ask him would he
stop Bartley going this day with the horses to the Galway fair?

NORA. "I won't stop him," says he, "but let you not be afraid.
Herself does be saying prayers half through the night, and the
Almighty God won't leave her destitute," says he, "with no son
living."

CATHLEEN. Is the sea bad by the white rocks, Nora?

NORA. Middling bad, God help us. There's a great roaring in the west, and it's worse it'll be getting when the tide's turned to the wind.

[*She goes over to the table with the bundle.*]

Shall I open it now?

CATHLEEN. Maybe she'd wake up on us, and come in before we'd done. (*Coming to the table.*) It's a long time we'll be, and the two of us crying.

NORA (*goes to the inner door and listens*). She's moving about on the bed. She'll be coming in a minute.

CATHLEEN. Give me the ladder, and I'll put them up in the turf-loft, the way she won't know of them at all, and maybe when the tide turns she'll be going down to see would he be floating from the east.

[*They put the ladder against the gable of the chimney; Cathleen goes up a few steps and hides the bundle in the turf-loft. Maurya comes from the inner room.*]

MAURYA (*looking up at Cathleen and speaking querulously*). Isn't it turf enough you have for this day and evening?

CATHLEEN. There's a cake baking at the fire for a short space (*throwing down the turf*) and Bartley will want it when the tide turns if he goes to Connemara.

[*Nora picks up the turf and puts it round the pot-oven.*]

MAURYA (*sitting down on a stool at the fire*). He won't go this day with the wind rising from the south and west. He won't go this day, for the young priest will stop him surely.

NORA. He'll not stop him, mother, and I heard Eamon Simon and Stephen Pheety and Colum Shawn saying he would go.

MAURYA. Where is he itself?

NORA. He went down to see would there be another boat sailing in the week, and I'm thinking it won't be long till he's here now, for the tide's turning at the green head, and the hooker's tacking from the east.

CATHLEEN. I hear some one passing the big stones.

NORA (*looking out*). He's coming now, and he in a hurry.

BARTLEY (*comes in and looks round the room. Speaking sadly and quietly*). Where is the bit of new rope, Cathleen, was bought in Connemara?

CATHLEEN (*coming down*). Give it to him, Nora; it's on a nail by the white boards. I hung it up this morning, for the pig with the black feet was eating it.

NORA (*giving him a rope*). Is that it, Bartley?

MAURYA. You'd do right to leave that rope, Bartley, hanging by the boards. (*Bartley takes the rope.*) It will be wanting in this place, I'm telling you, if Michael is washed up tomorrow morning, or the next morning, or any morning in the week, for it's a deep grave we'll make him by the grace of God.

BARTLEY (*beginning to work with the rope*). I've no halter the way I can ride down on the mare, and I must go now quickly. This is the one boat going for two weeks or beyond it, and the fair will be a good fair for horses I heard them saying below.

MAURYA. It's a hard thing they'll be saying below if the body is washed up and there's no man in it to make the coffin, and I after giving a big price for the finest white boards you'd find in Connemara.

[*She looks round at the boards.*]

BARTLEY. How would it be washed up, and we after looking each day for nine days, and a strong wind blowing a while back from the west and south?

MAURYA. If it wasn't found itself, that wind is raising the sea, and there was a star up against the moon, and it rising in the night. If it was a hundred horses, or a thousand horses you had itself, what is the price of a thousand horses against a son where there is one son only?

BARTLEY (*working at the halter, to Cathleen*). Let you go down each day, and see the sheep aren't jumping in on the rye, and if the jobber comes you can sell the pig with the black feet if there is a good price going.

MAURYA. How would the like of her get a good price for a pig?

BARTLEY (*to Cathleen*). If the west wind holds with the last bit of the moon let you and Nora get up weed enough for another cock for the kelp. It's hard set we'll be from this day with no one in it but one man to work.

MAURYA. It's hard set we'll be surely the day you're drownd'd with the rest. What way will I live and the girls with me, and I an old woman looking for the grave?

[*Bartley lays down the halter, takes off his old coat, and puts on a newer one of the same flannel.*]

BARTLEY (*to Nora*). Is she coming to the pier?

NORA (*looking out*). She's passing the green head and letting fall her sails.

BARTLEY (*getting his purse and tobacco*). I'll have half an hour to go down, and you'll see me coming again in two days, or in three days, or maybe in four days if the wind is bad.

MAURYA (*turning round to the fire, and putting her shawl over her head*). Isn't it a hard and cruel man won't hear a word from an old woman, and she holding him from the sea?

CATHLEEN. It's the life of a young man to be going on the sea, and who would listen to an old woman with one thing and she saying it over?

BARTLEY (*taking the halter*). I must go now quickly. I'll ride down on the red mare, and the gray pony'll run behind me. . . . The blessing of God on you.

[*He goes out.*]

MAURYA (*crying out as he is in the door*). He's gone now, God spare us, and we'll not see him again. He's gone now, and when the black night is falling I'll have no son left me in the world.

CATHLEEN. Why wouldn't you give him your blessing and he looking round in the door? Isn't it sorrow enough is on every one in this house without your sending him out with an unlucky word behind him, and a hard word in his ear?

[*Maurya takes up the tongs and begins raking the fire aimlessly without looking round.*]

NORA (*turning towards her*). You're taking away the turf from the cake.

CATHLEEN (*crying out*). The Son of God forgive us, Nora, we're after forgetting his bit of bread.

[*She comes over to the fire.*]

NORA. And it's destroyed he'll be going till dark night, and he after eating nothing since the sun went up.

CATHLEEN (*turning the cake out of the oven*). It's destroyed he'll be, surely. There's no sense left on any person in a house where an old woman will be talking for ever.

[*Maurya sways herself on her stool.*]

CATHLEEN (*cutting off some of the bread and rolling it in a cloth; to Maurya*). Let you go down now to the spring well and give him this and he passing. You'll see him then and the dark word will be broken, and you can say "God speed you," the way he'll be easy in his mind.

MAURYA (*taking the bread*). Will I be in it as soon as himself?

CATHLEEN. If you go now quickly.

MAURYA (*standing up unsteadily*). It's hard set I am to walk.

CATHLEEN (*looking at her anxiously*). Give her the stick, Nora, or maybe she'll slip on the big stones.

NORA. What stick?

CATHLEEN. The stick Michael brought from Connemara.

MAURYA (*taking a stick Nora gives her*). In the big world the old people do be leaving things after them for their sons and children, but in this place it is the young men do be leaving things behind for them that do be old.

[*She goes out slowly. Nora goes over to the ladder.*]

CATHLEEN. Wait, Nora, maybe she'd turn back quickly. She's that sorry, God help her, you wouldn't know the thing she'd do.

NORA. Is she gone round by the bush?

CATHLEEN (*looking out*). She's gone now. Throw it down quickly, for the Lord knows when she'll be out of it again.

NORA (*getting the bundle from the loft*). The young priest said he'd be passing tomorrow, and we might go down and speak to him below if it's Michael's they are surely.

CATHLEEN (*taking the bundle*). Did he say what way they were found?

NORA (*coming down*). "There were two men," says he, "and they rowing round with poteen before the cocks crowed, and the oar of one of them caught the body, and they passing the black cliffs of the north."

CATHLEEN (*trying to open the bundle*). Give me a knife, Nora, the string's perished with the salt water, and there's a black knot on it you wouldn't loosen in a week.

NORA (*giving her a knife*). I've heard tell it was a long way to Donegal.

CATHLEEN (*cutting the string*). It is surely. There was a man in here a while ago—the man sold us that knife—and he said if you set off walking from the rocks beyond, it would be seven days you'd be in Donegal.

NORA. And what time would a man take, and he floating?

[*Cathleen opens the bundle and takes out a bit of a stocking. They look at them eagerly.*]

CATHLEEN (*in a low voice*). The Lord spare us, Nora! isn't it a queer hard thing to say if it's his they are surely?

NORA. I'll get his shirt off the hook the way we can put the one flannel on the other. (*She looks through some clothes hanging in the corner.*) It's not with them, Cathleen, and where will it be?

CATHLEEN. I'm thinking Bartley put it on him in the morning, for his own shirt was heavy with the salt in it (*pointing to the corner*). There's a bit of a sleeve was of the same stuff. Give me that and it will do.

[*Nora brings it to her and they compare the flannel.*]

CATHLEEN. It's the same stuff, Nora; but if it is itself aren't there great rolls of it in the shops of Galway, and isn't it many another man may have a shirt of it as well as Michael himself?

NORA (*who has taken up the stocking and counted the stitches, crying out*). It's Michael, Cathleen, it's Michael; God spare his soul, and what will herself say when she hears this story, and Bartley on the sea?

CATHLEEN (*taking the stocking*). It's a plain stocking.

NORA. It's the second one of the third pair I knitted, and I put up three score stitches, and I dropped four of them.

CATHLEEN (*counts the stitches*). It's that number is in it (*crying out*). Ah, Nora, isn't it a bitter thing to think of him floating that way to the far north, and no one to keen him but the black hags that do be flying on the sea?

NORA (*swinging herself round, and throwing out her arms on the clothes*). And isn't it a pitiful thing when there is nothing left of a man who was a great rower and fisher, but a bit of an old shirt and a plain stocking?

CATHLEEN (*after an instant*). Tell me is herself coming, Nora? I hear a little sound on the path.

NORA (*looking out*). She is, Cathleen. She's coming up to the door.

CATHLEEN. Put these things away before she'll come in. Maybe it's easier she'll be after giving her blessing to Bartley, and we won't let on we've heard anything the time he's on the sea.

NORA (*helping Cathleen to close the bundle*). We'll put them here in the corner.

[*They put them into a hole in the chimney corner. Cathleen goes back to the spinning-wheel.*]

NORA. Will she see it was crying I was?

CATHLEEN. Keep your back to the door the way the light'll not be on you.

[*Nora sits down at the chimney corner, with her back to the door. Maurya comes in very slowly, without looking at the girls, and goes over to her stool at the other side of the fire. The cloth with the bread is still in her hand. The girls look at each other, and Nora points to the bundle of bread.*]

CATHLEEN (*after spinning for a moment*). You didn't give him his bit of bread?

[*Maurya begins to keen softly, without turning round.*]

CATHLEEN. Did you see him riding down?

[*Maurya goes on keening.*]

CATHLEEN (*a little impatiently*). God forgive you; isn't it a better thing to raise your voice and tell what you seen, than to be making lamentation for a thing that's done? Did you see Bartley, I'm saying to you.

MAURYA (*with a weak voice*). My heart's broken from this day.

CATHLEEN (*as before*). Did you see Bartley?

MAURYA. I seen the fearfulest thing.

CATHLEEN (*leaves her wheel and looks out*). God forgive you; he's riding the mare now over the green head, and the gray pony behind him.

MAURYA (*starts, so that her shawl falls back from her head and shows her white tossed hair. With a frightened voice*). The gray pony behind him.

CATHLEEN (*coming to the fire*). What is it ails you, at all?

MAURYA (*speaking very slowly*). I've seen the fearfulest thing any person has seen, since the day Bride Dara seen the dead man with the child in his arms.

CATHLEEN AND NORA. Uah.

[*They crouch down in front of the old woman at the fire.*]

NORA. Tell us what it is you seen.

MAURYA. I went down to the spring well, and I stood there saying a prayer to myself. Then Bartley came along, and he riding on the red mare with the gray pony behind him. (*She puts up her hands, as if to hide something from her eyes.*) The Son of God spare us, Nora!

CATHLEEN. What is it you seen?

MAURYA. I seen Michael himself.

CATHLEEN (*speaking softly*). You did not, mother. It wasn't Michael you seen, for his body is after being found in the far north, and he's got a clean burial by the grace of God.

MAURYA (*a little defiantly*). I'm after seeing him this day, and he riding and galloping. Bartley came first on the red mare; and I tried to say "God speed you," but something choked the words in my throat. He went by quickly; and "the blessing of God on you," says he, and I could say nothing. I looked up then, and I crying, at the gray pony, and there was Michael upon it— with fine clothes on him, and new shoes on his feet.

CATHLEEN (*begins to keen*). It's destroyed we are from this day. It's destroyed, surely.

NORA. Didn't the young priest say the Almighty God wouldn't leave her destitute with no son living?

MAURYA (*in a low voice, but clearly*). It's little the like of him knows of the sea. . . . Bartley will be lost now, and let you call in Eamon and make me a good coffin out of the white boards, for I won't live after them. I've had a husband, and a husband's father, and six sons in this house—six fine men, though it was a hard birth I had with every one of them and they coming to the world—and some of them were found and some of them were not found, but they're gone now the lot of them. . . . There were Stephen, and Shawn, were lost in the great wind, and found after in the Bay of Gregory of the Golden Mouth, and carried up the two of them on the one plank, and in by that door.

[*She pauses for a moment, the girls start as if they heard something through the door that is half open behind them.*]

NORA (*in a whisper*). Did you hear that, Cathleen? Did you hear a noise in the north-east?

CATHLEEN (*in a whisper*). There's some one after crying out by the seashore.

MAURYA (*continues without hearing anything*). There was Sheamus and his father, and his own father again, were lost in a dark night, and not a stick or sign was seen of them when the sun went up. There was Patch after was drowned out of a curagh that turned over. I was sitting here with Bartley, and he a baby, lying on my two knees, and I seen two women, and three women, and four women coming in, and they crossing themselves, and not saying a word. I looked out then, and there were men coming after them, and they holding a thing in the half of a red sail, and water dripping out of it—it was a dry day, Nora—and leaving a track to the door.

[*She pauses again with her hand stretched out towards the door. It opens softly and old women begin to come in, cross-*

ing themselves on the threshold, and kneeling down in front of the stage with red petticoats over their heads.]

MAURYA (*half in a dream, to Cathleen*). Is it Patch, or Michael, or what is it at all?

CATHLEEN. Michael is after being found in the far north, and when he is found there how could he be here in this place?

MAURYA. There does be a power of young men floating round in the sea, and what way would they know if it was Michael they had, or another man like him, for when a man is nine days in the sea, and the wind blowing, it's hard set his own mother would be to say what man was it.

CATHLEEN. It's Michael, God spare him, for they're after sending us a bit of his clothes from the far north.

[*She reaches out and hands Maurya the clothes that belonged to Michael. Maurya stands up slowly and takes them in her hands. Nora looks out.*]

NORA. They're carrying a thing among them and there's water dripping out of it and leaving a track by the big stones.

CATHLEEN (*in a whisper to the women who have come in*). Is it Bartley it is?

ONE OF THE WOMEN. It is surely, God rest his soul.

[*Two younger women come in and pull out the table. Then men carry in the body of Bartley, laid on a plank, with a bit of a sail over it, and lay it on the table.*]

CATHLEEN (*to the women, as they are doing so*). What way was he drowned?

ONE OF THE WOMEN. The gray pony knocked him into the sea, and he was washed out where there is a great surf on the white rocks.

[*Maurya has gone over and knelt down at the head of the table. The women are keening softly and swaying themselves with a slow movement. Cathleen and Nora kneel at the other end of the table. The men kneel near the door.*]

MAURYA (*raising her head and speaking as if she did not see the people around her*). They're all gone now, and there isn't anything more the sea can do to me. . . . I'll have no call now to be up crying and praying when the wind breaks from the south, and you can hear the surf is in the east, and the surf is in the west, making a great stir with the two noises, and they hitting one on the other. I'll have no call now to be going down and getting Holy Water in the dark nights after Samhain, and I won't care what way the sea is when the other women will be keening. (*To Nora.*) Give me the Holy Water, Nora, there's a small sup still on the dresser.

[*Nora gives it to her.*]

MAURYA (*drops Michael's clothes across Bartley's feet, and sprinkles the Holy Water over him*). It isn't that I haven't prayed for you, Bartley, to the Almighty God. It isn't that I haven't said prayers in the dark night till you wouldn't know what I'd be saying; but it's a great rest I'll have now, and it's time surely. It's a great rest I'll have now, and great sleeping in the long nights after Samhain, if it's only a bit of wet flour we do have to eat, and maybe a fish that would be stinking.

[*She kneels down again, crossing herself, and saying prayers under her breath.*]

CATHLEEN (*to an old man*). Maybe yourself and Eamon would make a coffin when the sun rises. We have fine white boards herself bought, God help her, thinking Michael would be found, and I have a new cake you can eat while you'll be working.

THE OLD MAN (*looking at the boards*). Are there nails with them?

CATHLEEN. There are not, Colum; we didn't think of the nails.

ANOTHER MAN. It's a great wonder she wouldn't think of the nails, and all the coffins she's seen made already.

CATHLEEN. It's getting old she is, and broken.

[*Maurya stands up again very slowly and spreads out the pieces of Michael's clothes beside the body, sprinkling them with the last of the Holy Water.*]

NORA (*in a whisper to Cathleen*). She's quiet now and easy; but the day Michael was drowned you could hear her crying out from this to the spring well. It's fonder she was of Michael, and would any one have thought that?

CATHLEEN (*slowly and clearly*). An old woman will be soon tired with anything she will do, and isn't it nine days herself is after crying and keening, and making great sorrow in the house?

MAURYA (*puts the empty cup mouth downwards on the table, and lays her hands together on Bartley's feet*). They're all together this time, and the end is come. May the Almighty God have mercy on Bartley's soul, and on Michael's soul, and on the souls of Sheamus and Patch, and Stephen and Shawn (*bending her head*); and may He have mercy on my soul, Nora, and on the soul of every one is left living in the world.

[*She pauses, and the keen rises a little more loudly from the women, then sinks away.*]

MAURYA (*continuing*). Michael has a clean burial in the far north, by the grace of the Almighty God. Bartley will have a fine coffin out of the white boards, and a deep grave surely. What more can we want than that? No man at all can be living for ever, and we must be satisfied.

[*She kneels down again and the curtain falls slowly.*]

STEP 3

DESCRIBE THE CONFLICT
AND THE PLOT

Although not all plays show two characters fighting over a woman
or a throne or one of their lives, nearly all plays show a conflict
of the protagonist with an opposing force—another character, the
law, nature, society. On your worksheet describe very briefly the
conflict of your play. Is it a lovers' quarrel, a family feud, a
murder? In *Riders to the Sea* the conflict is between Maurya's
family and the violent sea, or, more broadly, between humanity
and nature, against which people seem powerless.

By describing the conflict, you have partially described the *plot*
of the play, which, like the plot in a short story, is the cause-and-
effect chain of events from beginning to end. In other words, all
events in the play should be interrelated; each scene after the
first should grow logically out of the one preceding it; no action
should be included that does not result in another action
important to the play as a whole.

On your worksheet, list the main events in the plot of the play.
(See the sample on pages 122–23.) Your running synopsis of the action should make it easy for you to identify the most important
occurrences.

Not all plays include overt action and conflict. In plays concerned primarily with character, there may be very little action.
Instead, such plays concentrate on exploration of character and
revelation of internal conflict (see Step 5).

STEP 4

ANALYZE THE STRUCTURE

Most plays have roughly a "pyramid" structure: the action seems to rise to a peak of intensity, then fall to a final situation. Since the various elements of this dramatic structure appear in so many plays, they have acquired traditional names. These names give you a kind of shorthand vocabulary so that you can refer more precisely to the play you are studying. For example, it is much easier to say, "At the crisis of *The Proposal,* we can see that Natasha seems much like Lomov" than it is to say, "During the scene in *The Proposal* in which Natasha finds out that Lomov had come to propose to her, Natasha seems much like Lomov."

Following are the elements of dramatic structure that you can see in almost every play.

The *exposition* presents information about what happened before the play began and introduces most of the characters to us. In a long play the exposition appears chiefly in the first scene or two; in shorter plays it may be scattered throughout. In *Riders to the Sea,* for example, we hear about the deaths of Maurya's other sons, husband, and father-in-law in her speeches near the end of the play.

The *inciting force* is a person or an event in the world of the play that will change the life of the protagonist in some way. It usually does so by beginning the conflict of the main character (or characters) with the *antagonistic force.* In *The Proposal* the inciting force is Lomov's intention to marry Natasha. Technically, this is part of the *rising action,* the series of increasingly intense events of the conflict that build toward the *crisis.*

The *crisis,* or *climax,* is the turning point, the point after which the play can end only one way. In *Riders to the Sea* many readers think that the crisis comes with Maurya's vision of Michael and Bartley on the horses. The events that follow the crisis are called the *falling action;* this must lead inevitably to the end. This part of the play is usually much shorter than the rising action.

A comedy's happy ending is called the *resolution;* the ending of a tragedy is the *catastrophe.* At the catastrophe of *Riders to the Sea,* Maurya accepts the death of the last of her sons.

Although readers do not always agree about the precise point at which each of these structural parts begins and ends in every play, by thinking in these terms you can understand more clearly the play and your response to it. Look back over the play you are studying in order to identify its structural parts, and write them alongside the list of important events you made in Step 3, as illustrated in the following sample worksheet for *The Proposal.*

(Step 3—Main Events)	(Step 4—Structure)
Lomov tells Chubukov he wants to marry Natasha.	Inciting force
Lomov tells himself that although Natasha isn't ideal, she'll do to cure his nervousness.	Exposition
Lomov and Natasha get into terrible quarrel over ownership of Oxpen Field.	Rising action
When Chubukov takes Natasha's side, Lomov has nervous attack and staggers out.	
Chubukov tells Natasha that Lomov had come to propose, so Natasha says to bring him back and blames her father for the quarrel.	Crisis
Lomov returns, and Natasha tells him he was right about the property. Aimless conversation while Natasha is trying to bring up topic of proposal degenerates into another quarrel, this one about hunting dogs.	Falling action (repeats rising action)

Chubukov reappears and takes Natasha's side again.

Argument culminates in Lomov's fainting, which causes Natasha and Chubukov to think he's dead.

When Lomov comes to, Chubukov pretends (with Natasha's cooperation) that Lomov has proposed and Natasha has accepted.

Natasha and Lomov resume their second quarrel, as Chubukov says, "You can see these two are going to live happily ever after."

Resolution

Some modern plays cannot be analyzed in these traditional terms because their authors have deliberately rejected the rise-and-fall pattern. If you believe the play you are studying cannot be analyzed in the traditional way, note that fact on your worksheet.

STEP 5
ANALYZE THE CHARACTERS

As we saw in Section II, characters can be either "flat" or "round," either "static" or "dynamic." Since a play's performance time should not be much longer than two or three hours, a playwright usually has time to develop only a few round characters. Most likely to be round are the protagonist and, if the play has one, the *antagonist* (the character who opposes the main character). The less important characters are likely to be flat or *stock characters,* those who are so common in plays that they are easily recognizable as *types.*

Comedy is more likely than tragedy to have several *type*

characters. These can be classified in two ways. First, they can be classified according to the function they serve in the plot: for example, the *confidant* (*confidante* if female), or intimate friend, of the protagonist (like Horatio in *Hamlet*); and the *foil,* a character who serves by contrast to characterize the protagonist more fully (like Mercutio in *Romeo and Juliet*). Second, type characters can be named for their appearance and personality traits: for example, the *ingénue,* or innocent young girl, and the *villain.*

A playwright can reveal a character by using several devices: the *soliloquy,* during which the character thinks aloud onstage; the *aside,* remarks to the audience that other characters supposedly cannot hear (recall Chubukov's fourth speech in *The Proposal,* page 90); the character's dialogue and interaction with other characters; and what the other characters say about the character. Soliloquies are most often used in tragedy, where character development—especially of the protagonist—is more important than it is in comedy.

The protagonist of a tragedy is called the *tragic hero.* In earlier times the tragic hero had to be a king or a nobleman (Shakespeare's Macbeth, Hamlet, and King Lear, for example), because common people were not considered significant enough to play a role in a tragic story. Modern tragedies, however, have tragic heroes of any background: Willy Loman, for example, in Arthur Miller's *Death of a Salesman.* In *Riders to the Sea* all the characters are humble Irish villagers. According to Aristotle, the tragic hero is brought low because of a character trait—a *tragic flaw*—that makes the fall inevitable. In Sophocles' *Oedipus Rex,* for example, Oedipus' blindness results, at least partly, from his stubborn refusal to stop trying to find the source of the plague in his city.

Generally, we do not feel we know the characters in comedy as well as we do those in tragedy: that is, the *distance* of the audience from the characters is greater in a comedy. It is easy to laugh at a character who slips on a banana peel and falls if we know that character only by sight. If we have gotten inside the character's mind during a soliloquy, we cry rather than laugh at the fall. In *The Proposal*, although Lomov has a soliloquy in Scene 2, Chekhov keeps us distanced from him in several ways. Examine the scene closely to see just how Chekhov makes us unsympathetic toward Lomov. (Do not forget to notice what Lomov is wearing.)

While characters in a comedy must seem real enough for us to believe in their actions, they lack the stature of a tragic hero. Traditionally, the tragic hero, though defeated, compels our admiration; we feel awed at the spectacle of what a human being can endure, rather than depressed at the character's defeat. Because we react in this way, we do not feel that the ending of the tragedy is completely hopeless. Look again at the ending of *Riders to the Sea,* and analyze your reaction to Maurya's last speeches.

Choose a few characters in your play that interest you. Make a brief list of traits for each character, indicating in parentheses the lines, scene, or page of the play that reveals each trait. You will then be able to see which characters are round, flat, static, and dynamic, and you can label them accordingly. Here is a sample worksheet showing character traits of Natasha in *The Proposal* and Maurya in *Riders to the Sea:*

The Proposal: Natasha

Chubukov's daughter, age 25
Good housekeeper, educated, not bad-looking (Scene 2)
Tactless—shows she's not exactly thrilled to see Lomov (3)
Industrious—has been shelling peas before Lomov's visit (3)
Polite, on surface at least—asks Lomov to lunch (3)
Greedy, like father, over Oxpen Field (3)
Stubborn and sharp-tongued (3, 4, 5, 6, 7)
Dying to marry (5)
Surprisingly like Lomov—talks like him (5)
Hypocritical—tells Lomov he was right so he will propose (6)
A flat character: we see only one side—her worst. She's

---

static; the play is too short for her to develop. In fact, she's a type—the shrewish spinster who'll do anything to marry.

Riders to the Sea: Maurya

Old (everyone calls her that), and sometimes walks unsteadily
Religious—Nora says she's been saying prayers
Bossy—tells children what to do (they don't always obey)—but she loves them
Nagging, especially of Bartley about going to sea
Self-pitying—harps on her plight if Bartley is drowned
Stubborn—doesn't bless Bartley (but regrets this and goes out with bread for him)
Visionary, clairvoyant—sees dead son on gray pony
Fatalistic—resigned at end to death of all her sons
Round, fully developed, but static—play is too short to show any further development

Short plays often have no minor characters. In longer plays, however, it is often interesting to study a minor character in order to understand his or her function in the play. For example, the Nurse in Shakespeare's *Romeo and Juliet* is both a comic figure who provides relief from the tragedy and a catalyst in the tragic action. Here is a partial list of the traits of the Nurse noted by the student whose paper about the character is reprinted at the end of this section:

Romeo and Juliet: Juliet's Nurse

Earthy, talkative, bawdy, comic (Act I, Scene 3)
A trusted old servant (Act I, Scene 3, line 9)
Loyal to Juliet (II.4)
Not too bright(?)—impressed by Friar Lawrence's nonsense (III.3.159–60)

Stands up to Capulet (III.5.170–75), but then advises Juliet
   to marry Paris (III.5.279)
Underestimates Juliet's love for Romeo (III.2.85–90 and
   III.5.221 ff.)
Round and static

A very few plays have only one character. An example of this
kind of play is Eugene O'Neill's *Before Breakfast,* in which we
learn the whole story of two lives from Mrs. Rowland's *monologue*
(the speech of only one character; compare *dialogue*). As you read
Before Breakfast, using the techniques discussed in Step 1, notice
how O'Neill lets you learn not only about Mrs. Rowland but also
about her husband. Also notice how carefully O'Neill prepares
for the ending, which is a shock to us, yet seems believable because of the kinds of characters both husband and wife are.

BEFORE BREAKFAST

A Play in One Act

EUGENE O'NEILL (1888–1953)

   Scene. *A small room serving both as kitchen and dining room
in a flat on Christopher Street, New York City. In the rear, to
the right, a door leading to the outer hallway. On the left of the
doorway, a sink, and a two-burner gas stove. Over the stove, and
extending to the left wall, a wooden closet for dishes, etc. On the
left, two windows looking out on a fire escape where several potted
plants are dying of neglect. Before the windows, a table covered
with oilcloth. Two cane-bottomed chairs are placed by the table.
Another stands against the wall to the right of door in rear. In
the right wall, rear, a doorway leading into a bedroom. Farther
forward, different articles of a man's and a woman's clothing are*

hung on pegs. A clothes line is strung from the left corner, rear, to the right wall, forward.

It is about eight-thirty in the morning of a fine, sunshiny day in the early fall.

MRS. ROWLAND *enters from the bedroom, yawning, her hands still busy putting the finishing touches on a slovenly toilet by sticking hairpins into her hair which is bunched up in a drab-colored mass on top of her round head. She is of medium height and inclined to a shapeless stoutness, accentuated by her formless blue dress, shabby and worn. Her face is characterless, with small regular features and eyes of a nondescript blue. There is a pinched expression about her eyes and nose and her weak, spiteful mouth. She is in her early twenties but looks much older.*

She comes to the middle of the room and yawns, stretching her arms to their full length. Her drowsy eyes stare about the room with the irritated look of one to whom a long sleep has not been a long rest. She goes wearily to the clothes hanging on the right and takes an apron from a hook. She ties it about her waist, giving vent to an exasperated "damn" when the knot fails to obey her clumsy fingers. Finally gets it tied and goes slowly to the gas stove and lights one burner. She fills the coffee pot at the sink and sets it over the flame. Then slumps down into a chair by the table and puts a hand over her forehead as if she were suffering from head-ache. Suddenly her face brightens as though she had remembered something, and she casts a quick glance at the dish closet; then looks sharply at the bedroom door and listens intently for a moment or so.

MRS. ROWLAND (*in a low voice*). Alfred! Alfred! (*There is no answer from the next room and she continues suspiciously in a louder tone*) You needn't pretend you're asleep. (*There is no reply to this from the bedroom, and, reassured, she gets up from her chair and tiptoes cautiously to the dish closet. She slowly opens one door, taking great care to make no noise, and slides out, from their hiding place behind the dishes, a bottle of Gordon gin and a glass. In doing so she disturbs the top dish, which rattles a little.*

At this sound she starts guiltily and looks with sulky defiance at the doorway to the next room.)

(Her voice trembling) Alfred!

(After a pause, during which she listens for any sound, she takes the glass and pours out a large drink and gulps it down; then hastily returns the bottle and glass to their hiding place. She closes the closet door with the same care as she had opened it, and, heaving a great sigh of relief, sinks down into her chair again. The large dose of alcohol she has taken has an almost immediate effect. Her features become more animated, she seems to gather energy, and she looks at the bedroom door with a hard, vindictive smile on her lips. Her eyes glance quickly about the room and are fixed on a man's coat and vest which hang from a hook at right. She moves stealthily over to the open doorway and stands there, out of sight of anyone inside, listening for any movement.)

(Calling in a half-whisper) Alfred!

(Again there is no reply. With a swift movement she takes the coat and vest from the hook and returns with them to her chair. She sits down and takes the various articles out of each pocket but quickly puts them back again. At last, in the inside pocket of the vest, she finds a letter.)

(Looking at the handwriting—slowly to herself) Hmm! I knew it. *(She opens the letter and reads it. At first her expression is one of hatred and rage, but as she goes on to the end it changes to one of triumphant malignity. She remains in deep thought for a moment, staring before her, the letter in her hands, a cruel smile on her lips. Then she puts the letter back in the pocket of the vest, and still careful not to awaken the sleeper, hangs the clothes up again on the same hook, and goes to the bedroom door and looks in.)*

(In a loud, shrill voice) Alfred! *(Still louder)* Alfred! *(There is a muffled, yawning groan from the next room)* Don't you think it's about time you got up? Do you want to stay in bed all day? *(Turning around and coming back to her chair)* Not that I've got any doubts about your being lazy enough to stay in bed forever. *(She sits down and looks out of the window, irritably)* Goodness

knows what time it is. We haven't even got any way of telling the time since you pawned your watch like a fool. The last valuable thing we had, and you knew it. It's been nothing but pawn, pawn, pawn, with you—anything to put off getting a job, anything to get out of going to work like a man. (*She taps the floor with her foot nervously, biting her lips.*)

(*After a short pause*) Alfred! Get up, do you hear me? I want to make that bed before I go out. I'm sick of having this place in a continual muss on your account. (*With a certan vindictive satisfaction*) Not that we'll be here long unless you manage to get some money some place. Heaven knows I do my part—and more—going out to sew every day while you play the gentleman and loaf around barrooms with that good-for-nothing lot of artists from the Square.

(*A short pause during which she plays nervously with a cup and saucer on the table.*)

And where are you going to get money, I'd like to know? The rent's due this week and you know what the landlord is. He won't let us stay a minute over our time. You say you *can't* get a job. That's a lie and you know it. You never even look for one. All you do is moon around all day writing silly poetry and stories that no one will buy—and no wonder they won't. I notice I can always get a position, such as it is; and it's only that which keeps us from starving to death.

(*Gets up and goes over to the stove—looks into the coffee pot to see if the water is boiling; then comes back and sits down again.*)

You'll have to get money today some place. I can't do it all, and I won't do it all. You've got to come to your senses. You've got to beg, borrow, or steal it somewheres. (*With a contemptuous laugh*) But where, I'd like to know? You're too proud to beg, and you've borrowed the limit, and you haven't the nerve to steal.

(*After a pause—getting up angrily*) Aren't you up yet, for heaven's sake? It's just like you to go to sleep again, or pretend to. (*She goes to the bedroom door and looks in*) Oh, you are up. Well, it's about time. You needn't look at me like that. Your airs don't fool me a bit any more. I know you too well—better than you think I do—you and your goings-on. (*Turning away from the door—mean-*

ingly) I know a lot of things, my dear. Never mind what I know, now. I'll tell you before I go, you needn't worry. (*She comes to the middle of the room and stands there, frowning.*)

(*Irritably*) Hmm! I suppose I might as well get breakfast ready —not that there's anything much to get. (*Questioningly*) Unless you have some money? (*She pauses for an answer from the next room which does not come*) Foolish question! (*She gives a short, hard laugh*) I ought to know you better than that by this time. When you left here in such a huff last night I knew what would happen. You can't be trusted for a second. A nice condition you came home in! The fight we had was only an excuse for you to make a beast of yourself. What was the use pawning your watch if all you wanted with the money was to waste it in buying drink?

(*Goes over to the dish closet and takes out plates, cups, etc., while she is talking.*)

Hurry up! It don't take long to get breakfast these days, thanks to you. All we got this morning is bread and buttter and coffee; and you wouldn't even have that if it wasn't for me sewing my fingers off. (*She slams the loaf of bread on the table with a bang.*)

The bread's stale. I hope you'll like it. *You* don't deserve any better, but I don't see why *I* should suffer.

(*Going over to the stove*) The coffee'll be ready in a minute, and you needn't expect me to wait for you.

(*Suddenly with great anger*) What on earth are you doing all this time? (*She goes over to the door and looks in*) Well, you're *almost* dressed at any rate. I expected to find you back in bed. That'd be just like you. How awful you look this morning! For heaven's sake, shave! You're disgusting! You look like a tramp. No wonder no one will give you a job. I don't blame them—when you don't even look half-way decent. (*She goes to the stove*) There's plenty of hot water right here. You've got no excuse. (*Gets a bowl and pours some of the water from the coffee pot into it*) Here.

(*He reaches his hand into the room for it. It is a sensitive hand with slender fingers. It trembles and some of the water spills on the floor.*)

(*Tauntingly*) Look at your hand tremble! You'd better give up drinking. You can't stand it. It's just your kind that get the D.T.'s.

That would be the last straw! (*Looking down at the floor*) Look at the mess you've made of this floor—cigarette butts and ashes all over the place. Why can't you put them on a plate? No, you wouldn't be considerate enough to do that. You never think of me. You don't have to sweep the room and that's all you care about.

(*Takes the broom and commences to sweep viciously, raising a cloud of dust. From the inner room comes the sound of a razor being stropped.*)

(*Sweeping*) Hurry up! It must be nearly time for me to go. If I'm late I'm liable to lose my position, and then I couldn't support you any longer. (*As an afterthought she adds sarcastically*) And then you'd have to go to work or something dreadful like that. (*Sweeping under the table*) What I want to know is whether you're going to look for a job today or not. You know your family won't help us any more. They've had enough of you, too. (*After a moment's silent sweeping*) I'm about sick of all this life. I've a good notion to go home, if I wasn't too proud to let them know what a failure you've been—you, the millionaire Rowland's only son, the Harvard graduate, the poet, the catch of the town—Huh! (*With bitterness*) There wouldn't be many of them now envy my catch if they knew the truth. What has our marriage been, I'd like to know? Even before your *millionaire* father died owing everyone in the world money, you certainly never wasted any of your time on your wife. I suppose you thought I'd ought to be glad you were *honorable* enough to marry me—after getting me into trouble. You were ashamed of me with your fine friends because my father's only a grocer, that's what you were. At least he's honest, which is more than anyone could say about yours. (*She is sweeping steadily toward the door. Leans on her broom for a moment.*)

You hoped everyone'd think you'd been forced to marry me, and pity you, didn't you? You didn't hesitate much about telling me you loved me, and making me believe your lies, before it happened, did you? You made me think you didn't want your father to buy me off as he tried to do. I know better now. I haven't lived with you all this time for nothing. (*Somberly*) It's lucky the poor thing was born dead, after all. What a father you'd have been!

(*Is silent, brooding moodily for a moment—then she continues with a sort of savage joy.*)

But I'm not the only one who's got you to thank for being unhappy. There's one other, at least, and *she* can't hope to marry you now. (*She puts her head into the next room*) How about Helen? (*She starts back from the doorway, half frightened.*)

Don't look at me that way! Yes, I read her letter. What about it? I got a right to. I'm your wife. And I know all there is to know, so don't lie. You needn't stare at me so. You can't bully me with your superior airs any longer. Only for me you'd be going without breakfast this very morning. (*She sets the broom back in the corner— whiningly*) You never did have any gratitude for what I've done. (*She comes to the stove and puts the coffee into the pot*) The coffee's ready. I'm not going to wait for you. (*She sits down in her chair again.*)

(*After a pause—puts her hand to her head—fretfully*) My head aches so this morning. It's a shame I've got to go to work in a stuffy room all day in my condition. And I wouldn't if you were half a man. By rights I ought to be lying on my back instead of you. You know how sick I've been this last year; and yet you object when I take a little something to keep up my spirits. You even didn't want me to take that tonic I got at the drug store. (*With a hard laugh*) I know you'd be glad to have me dead and out of your way; then you'd be free to run after all these silly girls that think you're such a wonderful, misunderstood person—this Helen and the others. (*There is a sharp exclamation of pain from the next room.*)

(*With satisfaction*) There! I knew you'd cut yourself. It'll be a lesson to you. You know you oughtn't to be running around nights drinking with your nerves in such an awful shape. (*She goes to the door and looks in.*)

What makes you so pale? What are you staring at yourself in the mirror that way for? For goodness sake, wipe that blood off your face! (*With a shudder*) It's horrible. (*In relieved tones*) There, that's better. I never could stand the sight of blood. (*She shrinks back from the door a little*) You better give up trying and go to a barber shop. Your hand shakes dreadfully. Why do you stare at me like that? (*She turns away from the door*) Are you still mad at me about that letter? (*Defiantly*) Well, I had a right to read it. I'm your wife. (*She comes to the chair and sits down again. After a pause.*)

I knew all the time you were running around with someone. Your lame excuses about spending the time at the library didn't fool me. Who is this Helen, anyway? One of those artists? Or does she write poetry, too? Her letter sounds that way. I'll bet she told you your things were the best ever, and you believed her, like a fool. Is she young and pretty? I was young and pretty, too, when you fooled me with your fine, poetic talk; but life with you would soon wear anyone down. What I've been through!

(*Goes over and takes the coffee off the stove*) Breakfast is ready. (*With a contemptuous glance*) Breakfast! (*Pours out a cup of coffee for herself and puts the pot on the table.*) Your coffee'll be cold. What are you doing—still shaving, for heaven's sake? You'd better give it up. One of these mornings you'll give yourself a serious cut. (*She cuts off bread and butters it. During the following speeches she eats and sips her coffee.*)

I'll have to run as soon as I've finished eating. One of us has got to work. (*Angrily*) Are you going to look for a job today or aren't you? I should think some of your fine friends would help you, if they really think you're so much. But I guess they just like to hear you talk. (*Sits in silence for a moment.*)

I'm sorry for this Helen, whoever she is. Haven't you got any feelings for other people? What will her family say? I see she mentions them in her letter. What is she going to do—have the child—or go to one of those doctors? That's a nice thing, I must say. Where can she get the money? Is she rich? (*She waits for some answer to this volley of questions.*)

Hmm! You won't tell me anything about her, will you? Much I care. Come to think of it, I'm not so sorry for her after all. She knew what she was doing. She isn't any schoolgirl, like I was, from the looks of her letter. Does she know you're married? Of course, she must. All your friends know about your unhappy marriage. I know they pity you, but they don't know my side of it. They'd talk different if they did.

(*Too busy eating to go on for a second or so.*)

This Helen must be a fine one, if she knew you were married. What does she expect, then? That I'll divorce you and let her marry you? Does she think I'm crazy enough for that—after all you've made me go through? I guess not! And you can't get a divorce from me and you know it. No one can say *I've* ever done anything wrong. (*Drinks the last of her cup of coffee.*)

She deserves to suffer, that's all I can say. I'll tell you what I think; I think your Helen is no better than a common streetwalker, that's what I think. (*There is a stifled groan of pain from the next room.*)

Did you cut yourself again? Serves you right. (*Gets up and takes off her apron*) Well, I've got to run along. (*Peevishly*) This is a fine life for me to be leading! I won't stand for your loafing any longer. (*Something catches her ear and she pauses and listens intently*) There! You've overturned the water all over everything. Don't say you haven't. I can hear it dripping on the floor. (*A vague expression of fear comes over her face*) Alfred! Why don't you answer me?

(*She moves slowly toward the room. There is the noise of a chair being overturned and something crashes heavily to the floor. She stands, trembling with fright.*)

Alfred! Alfred! Answer me! What is it you knocked over? Are you still drunk? (*Unable to stand the tension a second longer she rushes to the door of the bedroom.*)

Alfred!

(*She stands in the doorway looking down at the floor of the inner room, transfixed with horror. Then she shrieks wildly and runs to the other door, unlocks it and frenziedly pulls it open, and runs shrieking madly into the outer hallway.*)

Curtain

STEP 6

ANALYZE THE LANGUAGE

You have already underlined or noted on your worksheet the lines of dialogue in your play that seem important (Step 1). You have also identified the various structural parts of the play (Step 4).

Now examine these two kinds of evidence together. Often the significant dialogue will point toward—or occur most frequently at—the crisis. In *The Proposal,* the crisis probably occurs when Natasha discovers that Lomov had come to propose to her and sends her father to bring him back. Note the language Natasha uses here: she feels faint, she groans, she claims to be dying—in fact, she sounds like Lomov.

Some of the passages you have marked may use *foreshadowing* (hints of what will happen). In *Before Breakfast,* for example, notice the references to blood that anticipate the ending of the play.

Whenever a significant speech seems to be emphasized, both by what it says and by its structural position in the play, examine its language closely. Use the techniques you learned in Sections I and II: look up unfamiliar words, check allusions, reshape unusual sentence structure if necessary.

If the play is in poetry, you may want to paraphrase some of the lines to make certain you understand them. You may also spot certain poetic forms embedded in the dialogue. For example, when Romeo and Juliet meet at the Capulets' ball (I.5), their speeches to each other are in the form of a sonnet:

ROMEO   If I profane with my unworthiest hand
   This holy shrine, the gentle sin is this:
My lips, two blushing pilgrims, ready stand
   To smooth that rough touch with a tender kiss.

JULIET   Good pilgrim, you do wrong your hand too much,
   Which mannerly devotion shows in this;

For saints have hands that pilgrims' hands do touch,
  And palm to palm is holy palmers' kiss.

ROMEO   Have not saints lips, and holy palmers too?

JULIET   Ay, pilgrim, lips that they must use in prayer.

ROMEO   O, then, dear saint, let lips do what hands do!
  They pray; grant thou, lest faith turn to despair.

JULIET   Saints do not move, though grant for prayers' sake.

ROMEO   Then move not while my prayer's effect I take.

Many of the important passages you have marked will contain images, rhetorical devices, and symbols. You should give these the same kind of attention you give to those you find in poetry and short fiction.

Sometimes you will notice a particular kind of *imagery* being used throughout the play. If you compare the various passages in which the same type of image occurs, you can often see the reason for the playwright's choice. You may also have material for a short paper (see Step 9). For example, in *The Proposal* most of the images are of animals, beginning with the description of Lomov as wearing *tails*. Some of these images are inevitable in a conversation about hunting, but the extent of the imagery goes beyond that. Look through the play again and list all the animal images you find. Does the surprisingly large number of them suggest that Chekhov is conveying some kind of judgment of his characters?

What kinds of images do you notice in *Riders to the Sea?* in *Before Breakfast?* Can you see any reason for the particular images used in each play?

STEP 7

BE AWARE OF IRONY

Dramatic irony (recall Section I, Step 3) occurs when the audience knows more about the situation than any one of the characters and therefore often knows what will happen as a result of the characters' actions. For example, even on a first reading of *The Proposal,* we know what Natasha does not—that Lomov has come to propose to her. So we are aware that she is ruining her chances for marriage by quarreling so fiercely with Lomov that he forgets all about his purpose.

More than one careful reading of the play, using the techniques discussed in Step 1, may be necessary to detect all the irony. Sometimes much of the play's irony becomes fully apparent only at the end. Examine the ending of *The Proposal,* for instance, to see how Chekhov manages several kinds of irony. Compare Lomov's early description of Natasha (Scene 2) with the woman we have met. Notice especially what else is going on when Chubukov makes his prediction of happiness for the engaged couple.

STEP 8

STATE THE THEME

In order to state the theme, the underlying idea, of your play (see Section I, Step 10), look back over the play and your notes. Then make a list of your ideas about the play. This should help you to articulate what you believe to be the play's theme. For example, your list for *The Proposal* might look like this:

Title is ironic, because Lomov never gets the chance to propose.

Lomov thinks only of himself, not of Natasha, in deciding to marry.

Natasha isn't in love with Lomov, either—it's almost the reverse of a love-at-first-sight story.

Conflict: between selfish desire of both characters to marry and their unwillingness to yield—either property or a point in a quarrel—to the person who should be beloved.

Crisis shows Natasha as the stereotype spinster who's determined to marry, and also reveals that she's a good deal like Lomov. (Note: we know why Lomov wants a wife—he tells us, and he includes every reason but love. Chekhov doesn't bother to give us Natasha's reasons. Apparently we're simply supposed to accept that women have no real life outside marriage, so they all want to get married.)

At end Chubukov makes a wry prophecy about the happiness of the engaged couple that we see is ironic because we see them quarreling bitterly even while Chubukov is calling for champagne.

Characters are all flat and rather horrible. Chekhov shows only one side. Yet we laugh because we feel superior to them.

Imagery is predominantly animal.

Theme: Some women are determined to marry no matter what the man is like; more generally, the blind, stubborn pursuit of self-interest ironically often brings the opposite of what would be truly beneficial, and we laugh at the characters because we feel superior to them.

STEP 9

WRITE YOUR PAPER

As with poetry and fiction, there are at least six basic kinds of papers that can be written about a play.

(1) You can write on a *single aspect* of the play: its use of *irony*, its *structure*, or its *imagery*, for example. In writing about any single aspect of a play, you should use the notes you made while studying the appropriate step in this chapter. One student wrote a theme of *characterization* about the function of the Nurse in Shakespeare's *Romeo and Juliet*. To do this, she looked back over the notes she had made in Step 5 (reprinted on pages 126–27) and used them to develop a rough thesis, outline, and rough draft, which she then polished into the final draft of her paper, reprinted on pages 145–47. Here is the remainder of her preliminary work, which resulted in the finished paper:

Rough thesis: In this paper I will examine the character of the Nurse in Shakespeare's *Romeo and Juliet* in order to find out precisely what her function is in the play.

Rough outline:

Nurse's characteristics
  earthy, bawdy, talkative, comic
  loyal to Juliet, trustworthy
  not too bright, somewhat insensitive
  round, but static; a foil to Juliet
Nurse's position in Capulet household
  old servant (has been there since before Juliet was born)
  takes care of Juliet, but has other duties too
Nurse's actions onstage in each scene
    I.3 listens to Lady Capulet talk to Juliet of marriage
      tells her husband's dirty joke
    II.4 goes on Juliet's errand to Romeo
    III.5 stands up to old Capulet

> keeps Juliet's secret (maybe she shouldn't have)
> but advises Juliet to marry Paris
> IV.5 discovers Juliet "dead"
> No more appearances; too much tragedy for Nurse's
> jokes
> Polished thesis: The character of the Nurse in Shakespeare's
> *Romeo and Juliet* serves as a foil to young Juliet, delights
> us with her warmth and earthy wit, and helps bring on the
> tragic catastrophe.

If you should decide to write a paper on the *theme* of *The Proposal,* you would concentrate on the analysis of the theme that you did in Step 8. Your rough thesis and polished thesis might then read as follows:

> Rough thesis: In this paper I will examine the title, the characters, and the language of Chekhov's *The Proposal* in order to determine the theme of the play.
> Polished thesis: Despite the fact that Chekhov called *The Proposal* a farce, and although we laugh in our feeling of superiority to its characters, the play makes a serious and rather depressing statement about human nature: people often pursue their own self-interest so blindly and stubbornly that they actually achieve the precise opposite of what would benefit them.

If you decided to write an essay on the *imagery* of *The Proposal,* you might begin in this way:

> Rough thesis: In this paper I will examine the animal images used in Chekhov's *The Proposal* in order to find out what they reveal about the human beings in the play.

Here you would use the work you did in Step 6, where you first noticed the predominance of animal images and listed them. Now you could classify them into two groups: images applied to or associated with the characters and images used in other ways. Notice which character is most often associated with animal images, and try to decide why this is so. What effect does this pattern of imagery have on the reaction of the audience to the character? What effect does it have on the play? Using the ideas generated by your answers to these questions, make a rough outline for your paper, and write a polished thesis statement.

A similar procedure can of course be followed for other topics. Write a rough thesis statement based on your worksheet. Then use the sorting-box method to arrange your ideas into a rough outline (see Section I, page 39). Work up a rough draft from the outline, test its coherence (as you did in Section I), rewrite the thesis statement, and write the final (or perhaps next-to-final) draft of the paper.

(2) You may choose to write a paper on *more than one related aspect* of your play: its imagery and structure, for example, or its techniques of characterization and irony. Here, too, you should use the notes you made while studying the appropriate steps to form your rough thesis and outline.

(3) If you have studied two plays, you may want to write a paper of *comparison and contrast.* You should begin by making a chart headed by the titles of the two works you are studying. Then list the points of comparison you want to consider in the left margin and, using your notes, fill in the sections across the page. Here is the chart used by the student whose theme of comparison and contrast is reprinted on pages 147–50:

Points of Comparison	The Proposal	Riders to the Sea
Opening scene	Lomov and Chubukov; short dialogue, gets right to point	Long, chatty dialogue before point is reached
Dialogue throughout play	Fast pace, quick transition, funny	Lengthy, slow, creeping to inevitable end
Final scene	Abrupt; engineered by Chubukov; problems not really resolved	Culmination of slow preceding action; no surprise; inevitable

The rough thesis produced by this chart might be:

> In this paper I will compare and contrast the techniques of dialogue used in Chekhov's *The Proposal* and Synge's *Riders to the Sea* in order to find out what they reveal about the effect of each play.

In writing a paper of comparison and contrast, you should use the *part-by-part* method. This method, which always keeps both plays being compared before the reader, is produced by moving across your chart, discussing each point of comparison with reference to each play before you begin the next point. If you move vertically down each column, discussing one play thoroughly before you begin the next, you will be using the *whole-by-whole* method. This method is often less effective, because it is difficult for the reader to bear in mind that you are writing about two works.

(4) Another kind of paper *explores a problem*. The student whose paper on the film *Death Wish* is reprinted in Section IV (page 181) let the problem investigated in the film become also the problem explored in his theme, but you might decide to explore another kind of problem connected with a work of literature. For example, you might want to explore the question: Is *Before Breakfast* a tragedy? Although it ends with the death of Mr. Rowland, you may have some reservations about calling it a tragedy (see Step 2).

Your rough thesis for such a paper might be something like this:

> In this paper I am going to try to determine whether or not O'Neill's *Before Breakfast* satisfies the definition of tragedy.

Then you might list the criteria for a tragedy (Step 2) and the aspects of the play that pertain to each criterion. You should be able to arrive at a conclusion, which will be presented in your thesis statement. The rest of your paper will be persuasive as you present reasons for your opinion. (If you are not able to come to a conclusion, your thesis statement will simply state that you will thoroughly explain the problem and conclude with the hope that your readers can form their own opinions on the basis of the evidence you have presented.)

(5) If you write a paper of *evaluation,* you will present in the thesis statement your own opinion of the play—or of one aspect of the play—and the rest of the paper will present your reasons for believing that your opinion is sound.

(6) A paper of *explication* is the type you learned to write in Section I. You will probably write this kind of paper only if you are studying a relatively long play. In this case you may decide to do a close analysis of only one short section, treating it as you would a poem. For example, passages that you might choose for explication are Juliet's speech of longing for her wedding night (*Romeo and Juliet* III.2.1–31) or Brutus' soliloquy as he tries to justify his intention to assassinate Caesar (*Julius Caesar* II.1.10–34).

If you write a paper of explication about a passage in a play, you must be able to tell why the passage is important enough to merit close study. For instance, the passage might show the beginning of the inciting force or the conflict. It might come at an important structural point—the crisis or catastrophe, for example. It might be important for the insight that it gives into one or more characters. Or it might show the playwright's skill in handling language or manipulating plot. Whatever your reasons for studying the passage are, be sure to include them in your thesis statement. Then use the techniques you learned in Section I.

In any kind of paper you write, you should make as many specific references to the text of the play as possible. Often you will want to quote a speech or several lines of dialogue to support your remarks, as did the two students whose papers on plays are reprinted on the following pages.

JULIET'S NURSE

SALLY YOUNG

Perhaps one of the greatest marks of Shakespeare's genius was his ability to take a stock character and, building upon it, create a round, human character with whom we can readily identify. Even his minor characters received this careful crafting, so that they not only spring to life before us, but also have a vital part in the working out of the plot of the play. The Nurse in *Romeo and Juliet* is a good example of Shakespeare's artistry in characterization. From the stock character of the nurse that appears in the Italian and English sources of the play, Shakespeare has created a character who serves as a foil to the young Juliet and whose warmth and earthy wit delight us, yet who is also in part responsible for the catastrophe at the end.

The Nurse's ostensible function in the play is that of servant in the household of the Capulets. Specifically, her primary duty has been the care of Juliet, although the Servingman's comment that she is "cursed in the pantry" (I.3.101) [1] reveals that she has other duties as well. Actually she is a familiar, trusted servant who has been intimately associated with the family for a long time, as her recollections of the weaning of Juliet show.

We get our first glimpse of both Juliet and the Nurse in the scene in which Lady Capulet first discusses marriage with Juliet (I.3). The Nurse's character is readily apparent here, unlike that of the quietly prudent, adolescent Juliet. Unlike Juliet, who is properly reticent in the presence of her mother, the Nurse is talkative; her memories of Juliet's birth and infancy take forty-six lines, despite a command of silence from Lady Capulet, a command that the Nurse feels free to ignore. Her recollections of Juliet's weaning and her husband's lame dirty joke reveal the Nurse to be earthy and even bawdy, in contrast to the innocent and unworldly Juliet,

---

[1] All references are to Shakespeare's *Romeo and Juliet* in G. B. Harrison, ed., *Shakespeare: The Complete Works* (New York: Harcourt Brace Jovanovich, 1968).

whom she characteristically advises at the end of the scene, "Go, girl, seek happy nights to happy days" (I.3.106).

This rather lewd advice is also tender in its own way and reveals the Nurse's great affection for her young charge. Here, as in everything else she says and does, the Nurse has Juliet's best interests at heart. She is Juliet's one true *confidante* and is trustworthy enough for the delicate mission on which Juliet sends her to Romeo. Despite her wordiness, the Nurse is loyal and tactful enough to keep the lovers' secret. She even stands up to Capulet when he is raging over Juliet's refusal to marry Paris, saying, "You are to blame, my lord, to rate her so" (III.5.170). But since she cannot tell Capulet why he is wrong without betraying Juliet's confidence, she does nothing to avert the coming tragedy.

In my opinion, the Nurse would have been justified in telling about Juliet's marriage under the circumstances. The fact that she does not reason this out shows us her intellectual limitations. Another revelation of these limitations comes when, after the deaths of Mercutio and Tybalt, the Nurse goes to Friar Lawrence's cell to find Romeo. The good friar lectures Romeo ineffectually, but she, impressed, comments, "O Lord, I could have stay'd here all the night/To hear good counsel: O, what learning is!" (III.3.159–60). Furthermore, the nurse cannot understand Juliet's high and pure love of Romeo, so when Juliet asks her advice, she replies,

> I think it best you married with the County.
> O, he's a lovely gentleman!
> Romeo's a dishclout to him . . . (III.5.219–21)

Ironically, this counsel, given to comfort Juliet, completely alienates the young girl, whom she loves so much, from her.

In a sense, then, it is poetic justice that the Nurse finds Juliet "dead" of the friar's drug, for by her insensitivity to Juliet's needs she has helped drive her to drink the potion. We last see the Nurse grieving, sincerely, but typically rhetorical and wordy (IV.5). Once Juliet is buried, the Nurse's role is fulfilled, however; there can be no place for her and her comedy in the coldly tragic catastrophe of the play.

Despite her shortcomings—indeed, in a sense because of them—the Nurse has a vital role in Shakespeare's play. She is not only contrasted to Juliet; she also provides a warmth in her affection for Juliet and some comic relief in her earthiness that otherwise would be conspicuously absent in the play.

TECHNIQUES OF DIALOGUE IN *THE PROPOSAL* AND *RIDERS TO THE SEA*

SHANNON DUDNEY

In studying any play we are concerned with where the action leads and how it gets there. A playwright must choose carefully the methods used to convey not only the action of the play but also the pace at which that action moves. Anton Chekhov and John M. Synge use similar methods but achieve totally different results in *The Proposal* and in *Riders to the Sea*. Both writers use dialogue between their characters to move the action, of course, but it is the difference in dialogue that achieves the precise effect necessary for each play to succeed.

The beginning of *The Proposal,* for example, opens with a short conversation between Lomov and Chubukov that takes us directly to the situation at hand: Lomov has come to ask Chubukov's daughter, Natasha, to marry him. Chubukov expresses his delight, goes to get Natasha; and already we are into Scene 2.[1]

Riders to the Sea, on the other hand, opens with the conversation between Nora and Cathleen, but instead of immediately leading into the key situation, Synge makes us listen to a great deal of exposition: the events of the past few weeks that have led up to this day. We must first hear

[1] Anton Pavlovich Chekhov, *The Proposal* in *The Oxford Chekhov*, trans. and ed. Ronald Hingley (London: Oxford University Press, 1964). All page numbers refer to the reprinting of the play on pages 89–104 of the present volume.

of a bundle of clothes sent by the priest, Nora and Cathleen's plan to hide the bundle, a discussion about whether or not "she" is asleep, and of the priest's having told Nora, " 'I won't stop him . . . but let you not be afraid. Herself does be saying prayers half through the night, and the Almighty God won't leave her destitute . . . with no son living.' " [2] Only after this do we realize that Maurya's son Bartley is going to sea and that she is worried sick because they still have not found the body of her son Michael, who has apparently drowned. It takes this long to find out what the plot is about, in contrast to ten speeches in *The Proposal*.

It is unnecessary to recount the plot of each play, but an examination of the different kinds of dialogue used by Synge and Chekhov is instructive. In *The Proposal*, Natasha and Lomov get into a stupid argument over a plot of land that Lomov says belongs to him.

"To us, you mean!" screams Natasha.

Lomov replies, "It's mine!"

Natasha: "It's ours!"

Lomov: "Mine!" (page 95)

The dialogue throughout the play is similar. It moves quickly with a brisk tempo, and transitions from scene to scene are just as fast. Scene 4 ends with Lomov's having forgotten all about his marriage intentions, but Chubukov speaks only three lines in the next scene to tell Natasha that Lomov had come to propose to her. By her eighth line she has made it all Chubukov's fault and screams to him to bring Lomov back. In three more lines the scene has changed and Lomov is back.

Chekhov uses only one line here to change the action again when Natasha says, "I'm sorry we got a bit excited, Mr. Lomov. I've just remembered—Oxpen Field really does belong to you" (page 99). All is well, and Lomov may get to his proposal yet—or so it seems. In twelve more lines, however, we have another argument when Natasha says,

[2] John Millington Synge, *Riders to the Sea* in *The Complete Works of John M. Synge* (New York: Random House, 1935). All page numbers refer to the reprinting of the play on pages 106–19 of the present volume.

"Father only gave eighty-five roubles for Rover. And Rover's a jolly sight better dog than Tracker, you'll agree" (page 99). It looks as though the two may never get together.

Finally Chubukov decides to take matters into his own hands, resolving the whole problem by simply saying, "Hurry up and get married and—oh, to hell with you! She says yes" (page 104). In the same kind of short, hurried dialogue that has occurred throughout the play, Chubukov puts an end to his headaches with the two. The situation is over almost before it has begun.

Riders to the Sea, in striking contrast to *The Proposal,* has a completely different pace or movement of plot. As the opening dialogue required many lines to get finally to the real point, so in the rest of the play the action moves slowly because the dialogue is so wordy and roundabout. We are almost certain that Bartley will not be dissuaded from his trip, but we must watch Maurya's attempt to stop him that goes on for almost two pages (109–10). The lengthy dialogue is almost a tug of war, which adds to our feeling of the pull within Maurya. Nevertheless, Bartley goes.

We have the feeling already that Bartley will not return, but we are forced to wait before we hear of his death. First we must watch the sisters' sending Maurya to apologize to Bartley, the sisters' opening the bundle of clothes and realizing that they are Michael's, and Maurya's coming back with the news that she has seen Michael on the gray pony that Bartley took with him (page 115). It is here that we hear Maurya's long lamentation and learn that her despair comes from the fact that the sea has taken her husband, her father-in-law, and all of her sons.

It is as though we are creeping toward an end that we do not want but that somehow we know is inevitable. When Nora and Cathleen hear a noise and Cathleen says, "There's some one after crying out by the seashore" (page 116), we know that Bartley too is dead. From here till the end of the play, Maurya speaks almost entirely a monologue, relieved only by the comments of friends who have gathered. It is as though we have staved off the ending as long as possible and now the inevitable has come.

The contrast with *The Proposal* is worth noting. In that play we go through what amounts to a ridiculous shouting match that is over before we know it because the dialogue governs the pace. It is short, snappy, almost terse. Comments are constantly flying: as soon as Natasha opens her mouth, Lomov has a retort. We almost feel as though we are doing the arguing because our attention moves quickly from one character to the other.

Synge achieved the opposite effect by using a different type of dialogue. We begin with a sense of doom to come. We move slowly from one character to another because each speaks several lines. The dialogue is long and hints at what will follow, but does not let us get there until the very end. We are forced to go slowly, to hang on to each line before getting to the next, to move at a deliberate, measured pace to the inevitable end. We are made to face the ending just as Synge's characters are.

Both playwrights used dialogue to move the action in their plays, but with completely different rhythms. Had Chekhov given long, drawn-out speeches to his characters, the comedy would have vanished and the absolute ridiculousness of the situation would not have emerged. By the same token, had Synge used short, crisp lines and hurried us toward the end, the impact of his drama would have been lost.

SUGGESTIONS FOR WRITING

I. Papers on one aspect of a work:
1. Animal imagery in *The Proposal* (Step 6)
2. Irony in *The Proposal* (Step 7)
3. Irony in *Riders to the Sea* (Step 7)
4. Irony in *Before Breakfast* (Step 7)
5. Human nature revealed in *The Proposal*
6. The attitude toward women in *The Proposal* (Step 5)
7. The attitude toward love in *The Proposal*
8. The role of women in *Riders to the Sea* (Step 5)
9. The function of the setting in *Riders to the Sea* (Step 1)

10. Synge's use of color in *Riders to the Sea*
11. The attitude toward death in *Riders to the Sea*
12. Religion in Maurya's world (*Riders to the Sea*)
13. Nature symbolism in *Riders to the Sea* (Step 6 and Section I, Step 9)
14. The function of the setting in *Before Breakfast* (Step 1)
15. Techniques of distancing in *The Proposal* (Step 5)
16. Comic elements in *The Proposal* (Step 2)
17. Noncomic elements in *The Proposal*
18. The structure of *Before Breakfast* (Step 4)
19. The function of Chubukov in *The Proposal* (Step 5)
20. The function of the priest in *Riders to the Sea* (Step 5)
21. The function of Alfred Rowland in *Before Breakfast* (Step 5)
22. A character analysis of Mrs. Rowland in *Before Breakfast* (Step 5)

II. Papers analyzing more than one related aspect:
1. Imagery and structure in *The Proposal*
2. Techniques of characterization and irony in *Before Breakfast*
3. Religion and plot in *Riders to the Sea*

III. Papers of comparison and contrast (see the student theme on page 147):
1. Views of marriage in *Before Breakfast* and *The Proposal*
2. Women in any two plays
3. Love in any two plays
4. Natasha in *The Proposal* and Mrs. Rowland in *Before Breakfast*

IV. Papers exploring a problem:
1. Is *Riders to the Sea* a tragedy? (Step 2)
2. Is *The Proposal* more than a farce? (Step 2)
3. Is *Before Breakfast* a tragedy? (Step 2)
4. Why does Alfred Rowland never appear onstage in *Before Breakfast?*

V. Papers of evaluation: Evaluate any play you are studying or any aspect of a play.

VI. Papers of explication: From any play you are studying, particularly a relatively long play, choose a short passage for close analysis, treating it as you would a poem (see Section I).

Section IV
Analyzing and Writing About a FILM

Although in connection with your study of film you may read a film script, you should remember that film does not exist outside the theater, and there is no substitute for seeing the film. For this reason, analyzing a film is different from analyzing any work of literature.

When you read a poem or a story, you can put down the book for any length of time and return to it when you wish. You can go back and reread a section any time you choose. The book is portable, the pages stay the same, and the words are fixed to the page. Not so with film.

Watching a film is like watching a play: unless you go to another performance, you cannot start it over. So your analysis of a film must be based on your memory of the multisensory experience you had in the theater. Reading the film script cannot adequately re-create the total impression of what you saw, heard, and felt, because the script was only the starting point for the finished product.

Included in this section is an excerpt from the script for Ingmar Bergman's *The Magician*. By reading it you can imagine the effect Bergman wanted to achieve. You can read the dialogue he wanted you to hear. But this experience is not the same as viewing the film. And because there is no way that a script can give precise directions for achieving a particular combination of "rhythms, moods, atmosphere, tensions, sequences, tones and scents" (Bergman's phrase), the completed film is often quite different from the initial film script. Each scene requires many different *takes* (different versions of the same shot), only one of which is included in the finished film.

Ideally, you should see the film you want to analyze at least twice. If this is not possible, read through the steps of this section before you see your film so that you will be prepared to spot significant details.

STEP 1
SEE THE FILM

Your first viewing of the film should be preliminary to the process of analysis. In this first viewing you will become familiar with what happens in the film so that on a second viewing you can be alert for scenes you want to study more closely.

STEP 2
NOTE YOUR RESPONSE

As soon as the film ends, analyze the dominant impression it has made on you. Has it made you feel happy, depressed, puzzled, nostalgic? Are you left with the feeling that all questions are answered, all mysteries solved? Or do you feel that you have been left up in the air, that questions have been asked that have no answer, problems remain that cannot be solved?

Write on your worksheet as accurately as possible just what your feelings are. This is important, because although you cannot control your subjective response to what you have experienced, you can put it in objective terms in order to understand it more precisely. Try to formulate your response as a sentence or sentences.

For example, here is the initial response to *American Graffiti* of the student whose paper is reprinted at the end of this chapter:

> Right after seeing *American Graffiti,* I felt shocked, because the ending told what eventually happened to the four main characters. Two of them were dead—one killed in a drag race and one in Vietnam.

Writing down your feelings may raise other questions about the film, which you should try to answer. If those answers raise still more questions, try to answer them, too. For example, the student whose response is given above added the following:

> The reason that the ending of *American Graffiti* was such a shock was that the scene just before it was funny and optimistic. I didn't expect the ending at all. It was the contrast between the two scenes that produced the shock.

STEP 3

SEE THE FILM AGAIN IF POSSIBLE

In this viewing you will be more analytical. You know already which scenes are memorable, so now you should try to figure out *why* they are memorable as you see them again.

Take some paper with you so that you can scrawl reminders to yourself of what you have seen. You will want to refer to these notes as you work through the remaining steps in the analyzing process.

STEP 4

ANALYZE YOUR RESPONSE

Look again at your initial reaction to the film (Step 2) to see if you want to make any changes or additions. For example:

> After seeing *American Graffiti* I felt shocked because Curt's last view of the white T-Bird—a comic and, in a way, hopeful scene—was so abruptly juxtaposed with the printed information about the characters ten years later. I was especially shocked to learn that two of them had died.

Your response to the film is based on your memory of it. More specifically, you recall images—pictures and sounds—of setting, events, and characters. The remaining steps in this section will help you to recall meaningful details of each.

STEP 5

ANALYZE THE EFFECT
OF THE SETTING

On your worksheet note the *setting* of the film. Is it the Roaring Twenties in New York City, the Romantic Forties in California, or Vaguely Modern Smalltown U.S.A.? Note also the details that revealed the setting to you. Some films tell the viewer what the setting is directly, on the sound track or after the credits ("Berlin, 1945"). In other films, the setting is revealed indirectly, by costumes, makeup, and props. For example, in Roman Polanski's

Chinatown the first clue that the setting is Los Angeles in the 1930s is the sight of electric fans in two sunny offices, indicating the absence of modern air conditioning.

From the worksheet of the student viewer of *American Graffiti:*

Setting: 1962, a city in California.

First clue to place: a car's license plate.

Approximate time obvious because of the old-fashioned cars and the styles of dress—long, gathered skirts on girls, white socks for both boys and girls, slicked-back hair on the boys.

Specific time—knew before I went: all the ads for the film asked, "Where were you in '62?"

Besides noting the general *setting* of the film, note how the *locations* (the places where particular scenes are filmed) help to create a particular mood or atmosphere. For example, the scenes showing the protagonist's stifling little family world in Bob Rafelson's *Five Easy Pieces* are set on a mist-shrouded island in the Pacific Northwest.

From the *American Graffiti* viewer's worksheet:

Several locations:

Mel's Drive-In Restaurant, teen-age hangout, crowded with cars and kids.

The Strip, where kids in cars cruise around for hours, yelling and waving at each other, the boys looking for girls and the girls looking for boys.

The canal, where couples go to park—becomes spooky for Toad when Debby, who has just told him about the mysterious Goat-Killer, disappears, and he is left alone in the dark with no car.

Paradise Road, scene of the drag race between Ferris and John, set in a wide expanse of empty fields—looks like the middle of nowhere.

The *locale* (the *where* of the setting) is probably significant if the film shows many views of it. For instance, in Jack Clayton's *The Great Gatsby* we see many wide-angle views of Gatsby's house and of Long Island Sound, with the green light on Daisy's boat dock barely visible across the water. Both of these images represent parts of Gatsby's dream—the first achieved, the other just out of reach.

Sometimes the film shows us the locale by using a *pan,* or *panning shot* (achieved by swiveling the camera horizontally), so that we get a panoramic view. For example, in Sir Laurence Olivier's *King Henry V,* the camera pans slowly from left to right to give us a view of London along the Thames River before closing in on the Globe Theatre. In a *tilt shot* the camera is moved vertically so that the view seems to move up or down.

But if the locale is not very important, we may scarcely remember it because the film concentrates on the characters by showing mostly *close-ups* (in which the camera shows us only a character's head) or *medium shots* (in which the camera shows us characters from the waist or knees up—and some of the background as well).

From the worksheet on *American Graffiti:*

> Contrasting types of locale seem significant. We move from the car-crowded drive-in and the Strip to Paradise Road, where the wide-angle lens shows us the smashed car in the middle of what looks like miles and miles of bare landscape. Then Curt's last view of the white T-Bird comes as he—and we—look down on it in the emptiness of California.

Is the film in *color* or in *black and white?* Can you see the reason that one or the other was chosen? Since color tends to romanticize its subject, *documentaries* (films of actual persons, places, and events) and other films intended to have a harshly realistic effect are usually photographed in black and white. A nostalgic view of the Old South, on the other hand, would probably be filmed in color. Recall the opening shot of *Gone with the Wind,* for example, in which Scarlett O'Hara, wearing a green dress that matches her green eyes, sits on the front steps of a whiter-than-marble mansion in an impossibly green, lush landscape.

Film *texture* can also be used to establish a sense of realism. For example, in *The Last Picture Show* Peter Bogdanovich used black-and-white film with a grainy texture, which gives the effect of a newsreel or a television newscast and adds authenticity to the events shown.

Sometimes a film uses both color and black and white for a special effect. In *The Wizard of Oz* the early scenes set in drab, drought-stricken Kansas are in black and white, while the magical land over the rainbow emerges in brilliant color.

From the *American Graffiti* worksheet:

> A color film—I guess for the nostalgia, romanticizing memories of youth, etc. Or maybe it just makes everything more vivid and bright—the girls' red lipstick, Curt's plaid shirt.
>
> I think when you remember good things of a long time ago, you always remember them as bright and vivid.

STEP 6
ANALYZE WHAT HAPPENED

Although not all films present a story in the traditional sense, most films do show events. Write a brief synopsis of the events shown in your film. For example, from the *American Graffiti* worksheet:

> The film shows one night in the lives of four boys who have just graduated from high school in 1962 and who are uncertain about their future. The events of the night affect

Using your synopsis, make a list of the important—because memorable—scenes in the film. Sometimes a film—particularly one adapted from a play—can be analyzed in terms of traditional dramatic structure; if this is true of your film, your list of important scenes may correspond to the traditional structural parts you learned in studying drama (see Section III, Step 4).

Whether you notice traditional structure or not, you should give particular attention to the *title* and to the *opening* and *closing scenes*. Sometimes the opening shots appear behind the title and credits and serve to establish a certain mood. In *The Great Gatsby,* for example, the credits are shown against a background of close-ups of objects in Gatsby's bedroom, including a black-and-white photograph of Daisy and a half-eaten sandwich. The viewer feels a sense both of death (the abnormal loneliness of these objects without people) and of life interrupted but continuing (a fly crawls on the sandwich). In *Goldfinger* the credits are shown on a *blow-up* (magnified image) of the gilded corpse of a woman, which will involve James Bond in a wild adventure.

Since the closing scene has the most immediate impact on your response and, in a sense, sums up the whole film, you should analyze it with care. In the ending of Arthur Penn's *Bonnie and Clyde,* there is a period of silence, followed by the slow-motion death of Bonnie and Clyde in a hurricane of bullets; the scene seems to last forever.

It is likely that the other scenes you remember are those that are important to the film as a whole: episodes that mark a turning point in the action or that reveal what a character is really like. The episode may be one of high comedy (Kid Shaleen's ride in Elliot Silverstein's *Cat Ballou*), gripping suspense (the car chase in *Bullitt*), joy and enchantment (Cinderella's transformation for the ball in the Disney film), or sorrow (Romeo's realization that Juliet is dead).

STEP 7

ANALYZE THE SHOOTING
AND EDITING TECHNIQUES

Words are used by writers of poems, stories, and plays to tell a story or communicate a mood. Similarly, techniques of filmmaking are used as storytelling devices. To the list of important scenes you made in Step 6, add notes about some of the techniques used to present the scenes, as has been done in the following worksheet for *American Graffiti*.

Opening scene. Mel's Drive-In in background as credits are shown. It serves as a kind of home base for all the night's activities.

Title: *American Graffiti*—writings on walls—seem so important and permanent—like life as a teen-ager, high school romances, boys and girls and cars. It seems, while you're going through it, that it will all last forever. But graffiti wear off—or are erased (scrubbed) off—the walls. The life we see in the film is in 1962!

Closing scene. Curt is leaving for college, seated in airplane, looks down at the white T-Bird, which, along with its beautiful blonde driver, has haunted Curt all night. Wide-angle shot shows car in middle of landscape, suddenly reduced (to size of an old, familiar dream?). Then shot of plane in blue sky and a slow fade-out (are we reluctant to leave Curt?). Then shocking list of names of the four boys and what happened to them. Coldly printed as though in a newspaper.

Curt's talk at the hop with young high school teacher who had gone east to a large university but came back to go to the local college. "I was never very competitive," teacher says. Lighting dim—scene takes place in side room of gym, away from dance. Medium shots and close-ups of Curt while teacher is talking—Curt is the important figure in the scene.

Curt tying rear axle of police car to post, causing police car to rush off, watching as rope jerks rear axle off car. We're with Curt under the car, because we follow him there with a tracking shot and watch a close-up of his struggle with the rope. So we know how he feels as he's performing the test to become a Pharaoh.

Toad alone in the dark at the Canal. We hear scratching, shuffling, vaguely ominous sounds (is it the Goat-Killer?) along with Toad's heartbeat—louder and faster as he gets more and more scared.

Curt's talk with the Wolfman, who conceals his identity as he urges Curt to leave home, to get as much out of life as the Wolfman has. Wolfman never stands up—he's trapped behind his broadcasting equipment. Wolfman gazes after Curt for several *long* seconds as the boy leaves the studio. Then cut to Curt looking into the studio window. Medium shot records his rueful expression as he sees the Wolfman resume his disc-jockey patter, realizes it's the Wolfman he's been talking to.

Drag race between John and Ferris. Accident, explosion— Laurie frightened so badly that Steve tells her he'll stay home and marry her instead of going off to college. Wide-angle shot makes people running toward car in enormous landscape look small and ineffectual—in contrast to car, which is shown in close-up and looks huge. Cars are more important than people, maybe, to John and Ferris.

The film cuts back and forth from one boy to another, to show all four stories going on all night.

> The film uses miniflashbacks throughout as it switches from one boy to another, so we live through the same hour four times. I got the feeling that the night was going to last forever.

Filmmaking techniques are of two basic kinds. *Shooting techniques* are ways of photographing with a motion picture camera, including various *camera angles* (positions from which the camera is aimed at the subject), *shots* (depending on the distance of the camera from the subject), *camera speeds* (rates at which the film runs through the camera; in other words, rates at which the action is photographed), and kinds of *lenses: telephoto* (magnifies distant objects), *wide-angle* (photographs a wider than normal area), and *zoom* (permits rapid change of focal distance).

Editing techniques are ways of cutting and splicing individual *shots* into episodes and scenes, including various kinds of *cuts* (quick shifts from one shot to another) and *fades* (*fade-outs* show the gradual disappearance of the picture until the screen is blank; *fade-ins* reverse the process).

These are the most basic shooting and editing techniques. There are many others. For instance, your film may give the impression of great tension and nervousness through one or more of the following techniques: *flash cuts* (sequences of very brief shots), *jump cuts* (in which successive shots lack continuity of action or subject), *oblique-angle shots* (in which the subject appears to be tilted), and *accelerated motion* (apparently abnormally rapid movement of the subject; actually results from a slower-than-standard photographing rate and a standard projection rate of the film).

Your film may suggest a dreamlike quality by using *slow motion* (apparently abnormally slow movement of the subject; actually results from a faster-than-standard photographing rate and a standard projection rate).

The *cinematographer* (camera operator) may follow an important character through a scene by using a *tracking shot* (taken with a moving camera).

The film may occasionally use a *dissolve* (the gradual replacement of one shot by another, generally with important corresponding images), either to provide continuity in the same scene or to convey the pictorial equivalent of a metaphor or simile. In J. Bronowski's documentary *The Ascent of Man,* the point made by a dissolve from a prehistoric spearhead to a modern nuclear missile of a similar shape would have required at least a paragraph of prose.

The film may handle the passage of time by using *flashbacks* (a shot or shots of past time inserted between shots of present time), often along with slow motion or *soft focus* (which results in a slightly blurred picture) to indicate the switch from the now of the film scene to the not-now and therefore not-real. A *freeze shot* (reprinting of one *frame*—a single photograph on the film strip—several times in order to suggest a still picture) can make a shot seem suspended in time—or in the viewer's mind. In George Roy Hill's *Butch Cassidy and the Sundance Kid* the freeze shot in the final shoot-out has a numbing effect, but it also leaves a shred of hope that the indomitable pair may have escaped again. They remain in the viewer's mind as they are last seen—immortal, legendary characters.

Music can be used effectively to evoke a certain mood, sometimes to establish an atmosphere for the whole film, especially if it is used at the beginning. Often this beginning music, or *overture,* is a *theme song* that is repeated throughout, sometimes in different keys or at different tempos.

Music can be used appropriately (lush chords for a love scene, discordant music for violence), ironically (the Beethoven symphony that accompanies the violent action of Stanley Kubrick's *A Clockwork Orange*), or prophetically (to give clues to the viewer that something—usually dreadful—is about to happen). Music can also be used as a *motif* (a recurring image) associated with a particular character or place. In *American Graffiti,* rock-and-roll music of the early sixties is heard throughout the film—at the hop, at the drive-in, on the car radios—typifying the period, summing up the characters' concerns.

Note whether any particular *sound effects* are used in your film.

If the gunfight lacks pistol shots or the car chase does not make tires squeal, you will not believe what you are seeing. These are expected uses of sound that you notice only in their absence. Sometimes, however, such necessary sounds are hushed so that dialogue can be heard, or they may be exaggerated to emphasize their importance (the beating of a terrified person's heart or the ticking of a condemned man's watch). *Overlapping sound* (in which the sound from the end of one scene is carried over the beginning frames of the next scene) is an efficient way of providing transition—building a bridge—from one scene to the next.

In *American Graffiti* we hear the sound of roaring car engines throughout. Whenever two cars meet, the racing of one car's motor issues a challenge to the other to drag—an effective anticipation of the climax at the drag race near the end.

Note the *lighting* used in your film. Light symbolism is so basic and familiar that we know how we are supposed to respond. Terror and evil are automatically associated with darkness: ghost stories take place at midnight; the vampire lurks in the shadows beyond the lighted window. Good things come with the daylight, however, and the ghosts and vampires slink away.

A film can manage our responses to light symbolism in the same way that a story or painting does. Comedies generally use bright lighting, for example, whereas most tragedies are predominantly dark. In Ingmar Bergman's *Virgin Spring,* a black-and-white film, the silvery heroine on a white horse stops in a forest glade, and we see the leaves of the trees as shadows on the rump of the horse. The witch-girl, seen in the dark forest, crouches over a giant sandwich that holds a toad.

In contrast to this traditional practice, realistic films nearly always use lighting that simply looks natural. And occasionally a film will deliberately reverse the accepted meanings of light and dark to shock an audience by confounding their expectations. In Alfred Hitchcock's *Psycho,* the murder occurs in a brightly lighted shower.

In *American Graffiti* the lighting is conventional and realistic, ranging from the early dusk of the initial gathering of cars and kids at Mel's, through the gradual intrusion of neon and headlights, to the early dawn of the drag race and the brilliant morning when Curt's plane takes off at the end. Inside Mel's is always the harsh brightness of fluorescent lights; and the scenes of riding along the Strip are dazzling, with car headlights seen in long shots and in glittering reflections in mirrors and on windshields.

STEP 8

ANALYZE THE CHARACTERS

As a film uses certain storytelling devices to let you know what happened, it uses other devices to manipulate your responses to the characters.

On your worksheet make a list of the important characters in your film, along with a few traits that you remember about each. Note the devices used by the director to present each character to you. Often you will find that the specific techniques you recall were used in the important scenes you listed in Step 6. Below is the *American Graffiti* worksheet for Step 8. Use it as a model as you make your own worksheet for this step.

> Steve, the popular class president, a "nice guy" in love with Laurie (Curt's sister).
> Except for white socks, looks much like any teen-ager today—hair not really slicked back, ordinary blue-checked shirt.
> Close-ups mainly in scenes with Laurie—dancing at hop, telling her they should each date others, agonizing during the wreck.
>
> Curt, central character, indecisive about going east to college the next day, called "wishy-washy."

The way the camera is used makes Curt the central character—many close-ups, point-of-view shots: when Curt was sitting on top of the car watching TV in the store window, I felt that I became Curt, seeing what he saw, only gradually noticing the three boys from the Pharaohs standing around him—and me.

When Curt left for college—same thing—I saw his hand being shaken as if it were my own.

Curt's clothes make him look a little square—bright plaid shirt, beige slacks.

Toad, small and funny-looking, innocent, "chicken" (I love Toad).

Scene outside liquor store, Toad asking man to buy liquor for him—high-angle shot shows his timidity and nervousness, makes him seem even smaller and younger—naive—prepared me for his being tricked by the man who takes his money, keeps liquor.

John, "Big Man," strong, his whole life is dragracing, he's champion.

Looks tough; white T-shirt, cigarettes rolled in sleeve. But—when John gets stuck with very young teen-age girl, his actions show that for all the tough exterior, he's a warm person: she asks if he likes her; in close-up we see his face, very embarrassed, as he tells her yes; he gives her his gear-shift top that she's admired all evening and follows that with a kiss; he then gruffly says good-bye as if ashamed of his display of affection.

Language especially good—slang of the time—"boss," "neat."

Are *costumes* and *makeup* used symbolically for a particular effect? Do they influence your reactions to the characters? In *Cat Ballou,* for example, the villain has a tin nose; in Ingmar Bergman's *The Seventh Seal* the actor who plays Death wears a black cloak with a hood that fits snugly around his bone-white face.

Are *colors* also used symbolically to influence your responses to the characters? The hero, wearing shining white armor—or a Stetson—usually rides a white horse; the heroine customarily wears a white dress. Be alert for a reversal of the traditional uses of color; in *Cat Ballou,* the white dress Cat sews so earnestly is not for her graduation or wedding, but for her execution.

How does the film let you get to know each character? *Shot distance* (amount of space between camera and subject) can be used to control the audience's sense of distance from and involvement with characters. A *close-up* of an actor, for example, shows only the face (an *extreme close-up* shows only part of the face) and may suggest to us that we are moving into the character's mind. In a psychological study of a madman, for example Fritz Lang's *M,* the film might use many close-ups and extreme close-ups, focusing on the actor's eyes or mouth.

Since *medium* and *long shots* show increasingly more of the character's body, more of the *locale* (see Step 5) appears also. Thus the film may reveal what is important to a character; for example, David Lean's *Doctor Zhivago* cuts several times from Omar Sharif in close-up to a medium shot of the actor in a Russian winter landscape. The same technique may reveal the relationship of the character and the world; near the end of Luchino Visconti's *Death in Venice,* the long shot of the dead Dirk Bogarde on the beach contrasts the brevity of human life with the infinity of the unchanging ocean. Or medium and long shots may be used in a comedy in which a director wants to limit the viewer's knowledge of the characters by distancing them from the audience. "Long shot for comedy, close-up for tragedy," was Charlie Chaplin's explanation of the fact that his films use mostly long shots. Likewise, if there is a risk that the audience will sympathize with the suffering of the wrong character, the director may achieve distance by using long shots or by putting some kind of barrier between the camera and the actor—iron bars or a closed window. In *The Great Gatsby,* for example, when Myrtle's husband is crying over her death, he is seen behind a window. Thus we do not feel intimately involved with his grief and can view him as monstrous when he fires his pistol at Gatsby.

In most shots, only the characters or objects in the foreground are kept in sharp focus; the background is less important, so it is photographed out of focus. In *deep-focus* shots, however, both foreground and background are kept in focus, to convey the idea that both are important. In Peter Bogdanovich's *Paper Moon,* deep-focus photography shows the little girl and her father driving along in the foreground and, with equal sharpness, the infinite background of dusty Midwest countryside—an effective means of conveying the isolation of the pair in a world to which they feel alien.

To let us know what a character is thinking, the film may use a *voice-over,* in which the actor's voice is heard on the sound track but the screen shows a close-up with motionless lips. The voice-over is often used for *soliloquies* in filming plays that were written for the stage. Sometimes the voice-over of a character is used throughout the film as the equivalent of the *first-person point of view* in fiction (see Section II). This technique is used for the Nick Carraway character in *The Great Gatsby.*

In a *point-of-view shot,* the camera lets us see what the character in the scene would see. In Mike Nichols' *The Graduate,* for example, a hand-held camera lets us move with the protagonist through a crowded room.

A cinematographer can use *camera angle* to convey what a fiction writer would put into words about a character. The higher a character's importance in a scene—or personal sense of importance—is, the lower the camera's position will be. A *high-angle shot* with the camera aimed down at the actor makes a character seem weak and insignificant. In Orson Welles' *Citizen Kane,* for example, we know that Susan, Kane's ex-wife, is dejected and has sunk low in life, as the camera looks down on her in the squalid nightclub.

Lighting is another means of manipulating audience response to a character. You have already noticed the use of light to tell the story (Step 7); now analyze its association with the characters. Shadows formed by a light aimed up at the actor can make a character appear sinister and villainous, as Kane appears in certain scenes of *Citizen Kane.* Light from above can make a character look spiritual, even angelic, as the sunlight does to Julie Andrews in the opening scene of Robert Wise's *The Sound of Music.*

Editing techniques you noticed in Step 7 are also used to show character. By careful *cutting,* the images in one shot can be made to intensify or counteract the effect of another. A kindly old lady in close-up looks gentle and reassuring until the film cuts to a medium shot of a skeleton hanging near her rocking chair.

Along with the techniques of characterization that are available only to the filmmaker, you should consider kinds of evidence that you also find in fiction and drama. Characters are often revealed through their *actions.* For example, the following excerpt from Ingmar Bergman's script for *The Magician* shows the servants' world in miniature and hints at Tubal's designs on the toothsome Sofia.

From the Screenplay for

THE MAGICIAN

INGMAR BERGMAN (1918–   )

Everyone sits down at the table and begins to eat in silence. The beer foams, the brandy glitters, the pies rustle and the big slices of bread fall softly. There is much chewing and swallowing; the glasses and dishes tinkle, faces blush. No one speaks, but the silence is filled with friendly curiosity. Tubal belches discreetly.

SOFIA: Bless you.
TUBAL: When I see these beautiful women with curvaceous figures, rosy lips and sparkling eyes, when I see these young men, fiery as young stallions, when I see our table sagging under all this abundance, then I'm inspired to say something about life.

He throws an enthralling glance at Sofia, who draws her breath so sharply that her corset creaks audibly.

SARA: How beautiful you speak, Mr. Tubal. Tell us more.

TUBAL: It's coming, my child. It's coming (*Drinks*) Life, I want to say, is a perfect performance of magic, with continually new and surprising effects.

SARA: Can you perform magic, Mr. Tubal?

TUBAL: Little child, let us not speak of supernatural things. Let us instead enjoy reality, which is considerably more natural, not to say more wholesome. That which is secret, that which is hidden, the ghosts of the dead, the vision of the future which hangs over us with its threatening dark face, all this we ought to leave be, my child.

SARA: Can you tell fortunes, Mr. Tubal?

TUBAL: Mr. Tubal *can* tell fortunes.

SARA: Read my hand, Mr. Tubal.

TUBAL: No, my dear child. You are much too young and full of hope. I don't want to destroy your curiosity, your joy in life, your naïve faith!

Tubal's voice takes on a clerical tone. The others at the table regard him with respect, all except Grandmother, who seems to have dozed off in the warmth of the stove and the steaming food. Tubal looks around and his glance touches that of Simson.

SOFIA: I'd say that one can really *feel* your supernatural powers, Mr. Tubal.

TUBAL: They are felt, they are felt.

SOFIA: A wonderful gift!

TUBAL: But heavy to bear, Sofia. And dark. He who has once sold himself becomes very lonely.

SOFIA: Oh my, Mr. Tubal, you make one feel both cold and hot under the corset at the same time. (*Blushes*)

TUBAL: One becomes lonely, Sofia. Hungering after tenderness and such things.

SARA: It's as if I heard our minister speaking. But more frightening.

SANNA (*cries*): I get so afraid.

SARA: What are you crying about?

TUBAL: Cry, my child! Her tears are like salve on the cancerous sores of an outcast from society.

SARA: Dear Mr. Tubal, tell my fortune anyhow.

Sara leans forward over the table, blushing with excitement. Tubal grasps her small hand and looks at her for a long while. She breathes heavily. Then the door opens and a large, heavy man enters. He is dressed in livery and has a pale, oval face, a drooping mustache and sinister eyes.

SOFIA: Sit down, Antonsson, and take your fill. This is Antonsson, Mr. Egerman's coachman.

TUBAL: At your service, Antonsson. We have already met.

ANTONSSON (*curtly*): 'Evening.

He takes off his livery coat, sits down at the short end of the table and pulls the brandy jug over to him.

SARA: Quiet now. Mr. Tubal is going to talk about the future.

Tubal holds the girl's hand and closes his eyes. At the same time he lets his other hand sink under the table and, as if by coincidence, fall on Sofia's thigh. Cautiously his hand makes an indiscreet investigation. Sofia Garp stops breathing and opens her mouth, but remains silent. In the meantime, Tubal has begun to prophesy with swelling pomposity.

TUBAL: I see a light. Now it is extinguished. It is dark. I hear sweet words of love. No, I cannot repeat them. My sense of decency forbids it. I think I see . . . I . . . Now it is beautiful . . . who can talk about decency at such a moment? Oh, it's stimulating. A young man. He rides at full gallop. It is beautiful! Nature itself.

Sofia puts her hands in front of her face, which is flushed with excitement. Grandmother has awakened and mumbles like a counterpoint to Tubal's melody. Sara is breathless; her cheeks are burning. Sanna cries quietly, leaning against Rustan, who sits with a sagging jaw and breathes heavily for the first time in his life. Simson, a handsome young man with moist lips and gleaming hair, searches Sara's face but she hasn't noticed him yet.

Characters are also revealed through their *speech*. Vocabulary and grammar, a foreign accent, a lisp can help us to know a character. We can also learn about the characters through what they say to and about one another in the *dialogue*. Here the believability of what the audience hears depends not only on the skill of the writer and director but also on the ability of the actors.

STEP 9
ANALYZE RECURRENT IMAGES OR SYMBOLS

Note the images of sight and sound that are used recurrently in the film. Here, too, you will find that many of the most memorable images are in the scenes you noted as important.

Are any images used over and over? Are they associated with particular persons or places? In Carol Reed's *The Third Man,* for example, the sound of a zither playing a certain tune always signals the approach of the villain. In Nicholas Roeg's *Don't Look Now,* the audience finally realizes during the murder of the hero that the glimpses of red seen throughout the film have been the cloak of the murderer.

Do the images *foreshadow* (give clues about) the end of the film or suggest additional symbolic meanings? In *The Great Gatsby,* for example, the major recurring images are those of flickering or wavering objects: a candle flame, reflections in water, a pulsating green lantern, even a wind-up phonograph tune—all designed to suggest the evanescence of the era and of the love affair. A dead seagull washed ashore beside Gatsby's boat dock foreshadows the tragic death in water of Gatsby himself.

From the *American Graffiti* worksheet:

> Recurrent images: cars, cars, cars—parked at the drive-in, in motion on the Strip, cruising and racing; we see them inside and out.
>
> And the sounds of cars—the gunning of the motor as a prerace challenge, the car radios blaring rock.
>
> Music throughout—like the cars—always the rock and roll of the early '60s.
>
> The cars become symbolic: they're the symbol of manhood and status to Toad, who thinks his whole life has changed when Steve offers to let him have his car while Steve is away at college: they're the same kind of symbol to John, oddly enough, who seems to be everything that Toad is not and wants to be. John's life centers around cars and his reputation as the best dragracer in town—a precarious position threatened any time another driver challenges him (with a gunned motor) to a race. The fact that Steve can so generously offer his car to Toad reveals Steve's maturity— just as Toad's actions on getting the car show that it takes more than a set of wheels to make a boy a man.

> Even Curt, who seems less involved in the car culture than the others, receives a kind of initiation into manhood by means of a car (the Pharaoh-planned trick on the police car that proves the bravery Curt wasn't sure he had and lets him know he could be a Pharaoh if he wanted to).
> The white T-Bird, with its beautiful blonde driver, tantalizingly glimpsed briefly throughout the night, becomes a symbol of an unattainable dream for Curt.
> Both cars and music foreshadow the end in the same way: both seem so permanent and actually last such a short time.

STEP 10

STATE THE THEME

Look again at the statements of response to the film that you wrote in Steps 2 and 4. Now that you have examined your recollections of the film in the intervening steps to determine what caused your response, you can state your response more precisely. For example, from the *American Graffiti* worksheet:

> American Graffiti shocked me into an awareness of the impermanence of life, which seems to last forever, but actually is no more permanent or enduring than graffiti scribbled on a wall.

Often your revised statement of response will include a statement of the film's *theme* (its underlying idea). Sometimes a character in the film will make a *thematic statement,* as Nick does in *The Great Gatsby* when he says to Jordan: "They are careless people, Tom and Daisy—they smash up things and then retreat back into their money or their vast carelessness and leave them for other people to clean up."

Many times the theme is not explicitly stated by a character, but must be derived from the images of the film as a whole. Whether the theme of the film you are studying is explicit or implicit, you should be able to state it if you first look back over your worksheets and circle the most significant notes. Copy these into a list, and then write what you believe to be a statement of the theme of the film.

From the *American Graffiti* worksheet:

> Time—1962—long time ago, yet seems vivid (color film)—as real and permanent as now.
>
> Title—significance of graffiti (Step 6)—seem important and enduring, but can be erased.
>
> Importance of cars (Steps 6 and 9): involved in life of every boy. Don't forget effect of crash on Steve—changes his whole life—he stays home, doesn't go away to college, and marries Laurie.
>
> Cars symbolic in two ways: means of initiation into (and representative of) manhood for all four boys; but also, like graffiti and like hit tunes in film, ephemeral.
>
> Miniflashbacks make night seem endless (time enduring forever) as we live through the same hour over and over.
>
> Music—rock and roll of early 1960s—all out of date now.
>
> Apparently hopeful ending—Curt's plane in blue, sunlit sky—then list revealing fates of four boys.
>
> Theme statement must include three things: significance of title, symbolism of cars, ending of film.
>
> Theme: As the title suggests and the ending of *American Graffiti* makes clear, teen-age life in 1962 (like all life anywhere) was as ephemeral as the music that filled it and the cars it centered around.

STEP 11

WRITE YOUR PAPER

When you write about a film you can write one of the six basic kinds of paper: (1) analysis of *one aspect* of the film; (2) analysis of *more than one related aspect;* (3) *comparison and contrast* of two films or of parts of two films; (4) a paper *exploring a problem;* (5) a paper of *explication* (you would probably write this kind only if you had a portion of the film script to study); (6) or a paper of *evaluation,* in which you evaluate the director's success in evoking a certain kind of response from the audience.

If you write a paper *exploring a problem,* you may decide to let the problem raised in the film become the problem explored in your paper. If the film offers a solution to the problem, then you should evaluate that solution. This is what the student who wrote on *Death Wish* (page 181) did. If the film offers no solution but you have arrived at one, you should include that solution in your thesis statement in the first paragraph. In the rest of your paper you will attempt to persuade your readers that your solution is valid, giving your reasons for it and supporting it with evidence from the film. If the film does not offer a solution and you are unable to arrive at one, your paper must state the problem in the first paragraph and then show how the film deals with the problem, referring extensively to the film and thoroughly explaining the problem. Your last paragraph might express the hope that your readers may arrive at their own solution.

The problem that your paper explores need not be one that the film itself explores. Instead it might be a problem related to the techniques of writing, directing, or editing used in producing the film. Your method here is similar to that discussed above: either you present your solution in the first paragraph and follow it with your reasons, or you state the problem clearly in the first paragraph and explain it thoroughly in the pages that follow. Again, your last paragraph could express the hope that your readers may find their own solution.

If you write an *evaluation* of the film—or of one aspect of it—you must consider the film as a whole. Your first paragraph, then, should include your opinion of the film and your reasons for that opinion. Look back over your worksheets and decide whether the details of setting, story, and character were effectively conveyed. Were the symbols an integral part of the film and used appropriately? Was the theme, even if complex, clearly evident throughout? Is the theme valid?

You might choose to evaluate the theme of the film and the ways in which the theme was conveyed. This is the kind of paper produced by the student who wrote about *American Graffiti*. In this case, use your work in Step 10, in which you evolved a statement of theme by considering all your worksheet notes and listing the significant ones. Your statement of theme should form your thesis statement in the first paragraph of your paper. From the notes that helped you make the statement of theme, make a rough outline to be worked into a rough draft. Then test the rough draft for coherence (see page 40), polish your thesis statement, and write the final draft of your paper.

KIDS, CARS, AND ROCK: EPHEMERALITY IN *AMERICAN GRAFFITI*

ELIZABETH BRYAN

On the surface George Lukas's *American Graffiti* seems as frivolous as the idle activities of the teen-agers it shows. Yet a closer examination reveals a more serious theme. As the film's title suggests, the lives of these teen-agers were as ephemeral as the rock music that filled it and the cars it centered around. This idea is underlined by the ending of the film, which shocks one into reality by revealing what finally happened to the four boys whose lives we have shared during the last night of their summer vacation in 1962.

American Graffiti brings to mind scrawled, haphazard writing on walls and fences, meaningless to a casual viewer, but very important to the writers themselves. Graffiti often tell of high school romances that are poignant and real at the time but usually fade into oblivion in a short while, just as writing on walls either wears off or is scrubbed away. The title is appropriate for the film because in it one sees the minds of typical teen-agers in 1962, oblivious to any problems greater than their own, completely unaware that the outside world affects them, destined themselves to endure the fate of graffiti, the fate of the cars they drive and wreck.

Cars, shown in nearly every scene, are the major symbol in the film. They are symbolic in at least two ways. As one of the most important aspects of the life of each boy in the film, cars become a symbol of status, the means of initiation into manhood—and several definitions of manhood are given. Yet cars, too, are ephemeral; nothing has less permanence than this year's model—which next year will be outdated and in ten years an antique. Cars dominate the film as a means of transportation for the teen-agers who gather at Mel's Drive-In and then ritualistically cruise the Strip, making contacts, picking up dates, setting up races.

Cars are most important to the two boys in the film who seem most unlike. John is "Big Man," the dragracing champion who realizes the precariousness of his position every time a challenger guns the motor of his car, his tough exterior shown by the cigarette package rolled in his shirt sleeve, yet who is able to act gently, even gallantly toward the young girl he gets stuck with for the night. Toad is the bespectacled high school junior who thinks his whole life will change now that he's inherited the car of his friend who's leaving for college, yet who finds that it takes more than four wheels to make a boy a man. A car is only a false symbol of manhood, Toad learns, when his underage attempt to buy liquor fails, and he's cheated of his money as well as his newly acquired self-respect. His naive insecurity and timidity are most apparent during the liquor store scene, in which a high-angle shot makes him look small and insignificant.

Toad's friend who has given him use of the car is Steve, whose comparative maturity is shown not only by his conservative dress and nice-guy, class-president image, but also by his ability to relinquish his car, so important a status symbol to his friends. But Steve's life is changed by means of a car during the last vacation night. He has tried to break with his steady girl Laurie before he leaves her to go to college, but she's involved in the smash-up of a racing car. The importance of the wrecked car is shown by its prominence in a deep-focus shot; it dwarfs the small, ineffectual humans who run toward it. The terrified Laurie begs Steve not to leave her. He readily abandons his plans to leave. Perhaps he welcomes the excuse to stay.

To Curt, the character from whose point of view we see most of the film, cars seem relatively unimportant. Yet it's a trick played on a police car that qualifies Curt to join the Pharaohs gang if he wants to, that initiates him into the world of the brave and the competitive, that perhaps is the final factor tipping the scales toward his decision to go to college after all. "I was never very competitive," his former high school teacher tells him, "but you should go out into the world and do things." "Maybe I'm not competitive either," Curt replies, really not knowing; but the car initiation shows him that he can be, and he leaves for college the next morning with that knowledge.

During that last long vacation night on the Strip—made to seem longer by the use of miniflashbacks that make us relive the same hour four times—Curt is haunted by glimpses of a white T-Bird and its beautiful blonde driver. Curt never gets any closer to this vision than the length of a city block, but the T-Bird is the last thing he sees from the plane window as he leaves for college the next morning. The white T-Bird seems to symbolize Curt's unattainable dream, and yet he's leaving it, he's not being abandoned or destroyed, and our view of his plane in the blue, sunlit sky of morning is a hopeful and appropriate ending for a story about four basically good American guys.

Except it's not the ending. Immediately after the scene, there's a slow fade-out and then the real ending, a shocking one that jolts us from the pretty-colored, nostalgic trip we've been on to the harsh reality of the world of Now. We see a picture of each boy along with a newspaperlike listing of what happened to him. Steve sells insurance in California; he married Laurie, of course, and missed the adventure of his generation. Curt is a writer, living in Canada; we guess that he is a draft evader and that he has written this story. John and Toad are both dead, the first killed in a drag race (of course), the second in Vietnam.

Like graffiti on a wall in 1962, like the music that blared from the jukebox in Mel's Drive-In, like the cars that have all been driven to junk—youth passes, people change, life ends.

DEATH WISH:
WHAT'S WRONG WITH BEING A VIGILANTE?

REN DECATUR

Few films dealing with contemporary, controversial issues offer feasible solutions. Most merely reflect the hopeless dilemmas that continue to perplex humanity. The Dino de Laurentiis production of Brian Garfield's novel *Death Wish* seems at first to be an exception. The question posed in the film is simple: In the face of the skyrocketing crime rate and the apparent helplessness of city police, why can't individuals protect themselves against criminal acts? Paul Kersey, a middle-aged development engineer living in New York City and the hero of *Death Wish,* believes that he can.

As a result of a brutal attack by three muggers, Kersey's wife is killed and his daughter institutionalized in a state of schizoid, paranoid shock. In questioning the police detective in charge of the investigation, Kersey asks if there is a chance of apprehending the muggers. The detective replies that there is a chance. "Just a chance?" asks Kersey. "I'd be less than honest if I said more, Mr. Kersey. In the city that's the way it is."

Kersey, embracing the notion that self-protection is the best, perhaps the only, deterrent to criminal acts against private citizens, acquires a gun and places himself in situations that will attract muggers. Always in self-defense, Kersey thwarts several muggings by shooting and killing his assailants. The press—and public—learn of his actions and label him "the vigilante." Police officials designate an entire detail to investigate the actions of the vigilante. The irony of the police devoting untold man-hours to pursue the investigation of the vigilante instead of taking similar measures to stop the muggings is obvious. Director Michael Winner focuses upon meetings of the police detail assigned to the vigilante killings and cuts, in effective contrast, to the actions of Kersey.

Kersey is finally caught, but rather than prosecute him, the chief of police simply demands that he leave New York. The vigilante is transferred to Chicago, where as the film ends we see him silently indicate his intention to continue his own campaign against crime in our cities.

As this synopsis indicates, the social commentary in the film is extensive and firmly based in reality. Other American films that have attempted realistic social commentary have failed because not all segments of society could fully identify with the problems shown. Such films lacked what I shall call "identity transition": a transition through social and economic levels allowing anyone to identify with the proper characters. Identity transition requires that the film director effectively communicate the characters' situation to the majority of the general viewing public, regardless of their social and economic status. If identity transition is provided in a film, the impact of the film will be felt by everyone who sees it. The reaction "Such violence is deplorable but could never happen to me" does not occur if identity transition is effective. No one who sees *Death Wish* can fail to acknowledge that what happened to the Kersey family can happen to anyone.

There are, of course, those who contend that violence begets violence and who are, therefore, against vigilante, self-protective measures. Perhaps this is true when we deal with rational persons, but, as Winner shows by skillful use of extreme close-ups, we cannot always assume that we are dealing with rational, psychologically balanced human beings. In view of this fact, the alternatives open to us for stemming the ever-increasing tide of crime in our cities seem frighteningly limited.

Death Wish does not pretend that its solution to the problem of violence is the definitive one. Yet it comes dangerously close to making its solution seem definitive for many viewers.[1] In its convincing demonstration that simple deterrents to crime can be effective, it seems to show that answers to complex problems are possibly more simple than the problems themselves might lead us to believe. Admittedly, in a technologically advanced society it is shameful that in addition to the threats of economic chaos, ecological disaster, and nuclear holocaust, we must also fear for our personal safety, even in our own homes. Yet are we ready for a population made up of vigilantes? It is this question that *Death Wish,* in appearing to show a quick and simple answer to the problem of violence in our cities, really evades.

[1] See Timothy P. Meyer and James A. Anderson, "Media Violence Research: Interpreting the Findings," *Journal of Broadcasting,* 17 (Fall, 1973), pp. 447–58.

SUGGESTIONS FOR WRITING

I. Papers analyzing one aspect:
  1. The editing, photography, lighting, or sound in any film (Steps 5, 6, 7, 8)
  2. Techniques of characterization in any film (Step 8)
II. Papers analyzing more than one related aspect:
  1. Makeup, costumes, and acting (Step 8)
  2. Lighting and setting (Steps 5, 6, 7, 8)
III. Papers of comparison and contrast:
  1. *Butch Cassidy and the Sundance Kid* and *Easy Rider*
  2. *American Graffiti* and *The Last Picture Show*
  3. *The Sting* and *California Split*
  4. Any two similar films by the same director: Alfred Hitchcock, Ingmar Bergman, Federico Fellini

5. Any two similar films starring the same actor: Humphrey Bogart, Greta Garbo, Sir Laurence Olivier

IV. Papers exploring a problem (see the student paper on page 181):
1. For any film, did the setting and acting adequately support the plot?
2. For any film, was the choice of color or black and white film appropriate?
3. If the film was based on a novel (for example, Peter Bogdanovich's *Daisy Miller*, Luchino Visconti's *Death in Venice*), was the impact of the novel adequately transferred to the screen?

V. Papers of explication: Choose for explication any portion of any film you are studying if you also have the film script. If you can see the film, you might want to explicate the passage from Ingmar Bergman's *The Magician* reprinted on pages 170–73.

VI. Paper of evaluation of any film.

VII. Paper on the theme of any film (see the student paper on page 178).

DOCUMENTATION CHECKLIST

Techniques of documentation have been illustrated for you in the student papers. Additional—even alternative—techniques exist, and we suggest that you ask your instructor to recommend a guide to documentation. Many handbooks used in composition classes include guidelines for writing and documenting papers; in addition, the *MLA Style Sheet*, 2nd ed. (1970), is recommended.

Below are some sample footnotes and bibliography entries, followed by Richard A. Davis' Footnote Checklist. It will be useful for you to read your footnotes against the questions in the checklist to ensure that you have included all pertinent information.

FOOTNOTES

[1] Sophocles, *Agamemnon*, in *Ten Greek Plays in Contemporary Translation*, ed. L. R. Lind (Boston: Houghton Mifflin, Riverside Editions, 1957), p. 55.
[2] Oliver Goldsmith, "The Deserted Village," in *The Vicar of Wakefield and Other Writings*, ed. Frederick W. Hilles, The Modern Library (New York: Random House, 1955), p. 467.
[3] Christopher Isherwood, "The Last of Mr. Norris," in *The Berlin Stories* (New York: New Directions, 1963), p. 80.

BIBLIOGRAPHY

Baugh, Albert C. *A Literary History of England.* New York: Appleton-Century-Crofts, 1967.

Bryan, Margaret B. "Swift's Use of the Looking-Glass in *Gulliver's Travels,*" *Connecticut Review,* 8 (1974), 90–94.

Davis, Boyd H. "Review of *The Neogrammarians: A Re-evaluation of Their Place in the Development of Linguistic Science,* by Kurt R. Jankowsky." *Historiographia Linguistica,* 1 (1973), 95–110.

Isherwood, Christopher. *The Berlin Stories.* New York: New Directions, 1963.

CHECKLIST

1. Use the following checklist for a footnote citing a BOOK.
   a. Author data: Do I have
      —first, middle, last names, followed by a comma?
      (If "author" is really "editor[s]," do I have ed. or eds.?)
   b. Book data: Do I have
      —the *full* title, underlined?
      —the number of volumes (if more than one)?
      —edition number (if other than first)?
   c. Publication data: Do I have
      —within parentheses: place followed by a colon?
                              publisher followed by a comma?
                              date?
   d. Specific reference data: Do I have
      —the volume number (if necessary)?
      —the correct page number(s), followed by a period?
2. Use the following checklist for a footnote citing an ARTICLE.
   a. Author data: Do I have
      —first, middle, last names, followed by a comma?

b. Article data: Do I have
   —double quotation marks, the full title of the article, a comma, and double quotation marks again?
   —the name of the periodical, underlined?
c. Publication data: Do I have
   —the volume of the periodical?
   —parentheses enclosing the date of the periodical: (January, 1968)?
d. Specific reference data: Do I have
   —the correct page number(s) followed by a period?

INDEX

A 5
B 6
C 7
D 8
E 9
F 0
G 1
H 2
I 3
J 4